Better Homes & Gardens

CHRISTMAS COOKING
FROM THE HEART™

Embrace the Season

Meredith Consumer Marketing
Des Moines, Iowa

CHRISTMAS COOKING
FROM THE HEART™

MEREDITH CORPORATION CONSUMER MARKETING
Director of Direct Marketing-Books: Daniel Fagan
Marketing Operations Manager: Max Daily
Assistant Marketing Manager: Kylie Dazzo
Content Manager: Julie Doll
Senior Production Manager: Liza Ward

WATERBURY PUBLICATIONS, INC.
Editorial Director: Lisa Kingsley
Creative Director: Ken Carlson
Associate Editor: Tricia Bergman
Associate Editor: Maggie Glisan
Associate Design Director: Doug Samuelson
Production Assistant: Mindy Samuelson
Contributing Copy Editor: Peg Smith
Contributing Proofreader: Carrie Truesdell
Contributing Food Stylist: Jennifer Peterson

***BETTER HOMES & GARDENS*® MAGAZINE**
Editor in Chief: Stephen Orr
Creative Director: Jennifer D. Madara
Executive Editor: Oma Blaise Ford

MEREDITH CORPORATION
President and CEO: Tom Harty
Chairman: Stephen M. Lacy
Vice Chairman: Mell Meredith Frazier

Copyright © 2021 by Meredith Corporation.
Des Moines, Iowa.
First Edition. All rights reserved.
Printed in the United States of America.
ISSN: 1083-4451   ISBN: 978-0-696-30309-8

Better Homes & Gardens

TEST KITCHEN

Our seal assures you that every recipe in *Christmas Cooking from the Heart*™ has been tested in the *Better Homes & Gardens*® Test Kitchen. This means that each recipe is practical and reliable, and it meets our high standards of taste appeal. We guarantee your satisfaction with this book for as long as you own it.

All of us at Meredith Consumer Marketing are dedicated to providing you with information and ideas to enhance your home. We welcome your comments and suggestions. Write to us at: Meredith Consumer Marketing, 1716 Locust St, Des Moines, IA 50309-3023. *Christmas Cooking from the Heart*™ is available by mail. To order editions from past years, call 800/627-5490.

Cover: Champagne Cake
(recipe, page 80)

MINIATURE ORANGE-
CRANBERRY CAKES,
PAGE 79

COLD ROASTED SALMON,
PAGE 137

Table of Contents

Embrace the Season

Some of the best memories are made at the table or in the kitchen, surrounded by family and friends. Whether you entertain at holiday gatherings, host houseguests, or bake cookies and breads for neighbors and co-workers, dependable and flavorful recipes are a must.

And that's what *Better Homes & Gardens® Christmas Cooking from the Heart™* is all about—providing delicious recipes that will help you create wonderful experiences this Christmas and memories for holidays to come. Get inspired with intriguing recipes for a large gathering around the table: Pan-Roasted Beef Tenderloin with Mushrooms (page 10); Roasted Potatoes, Fennel and Lemon (page 18); and Curried Celery Soup with Pear (page 24). For gift-giving, treat fortunate recipients to Caramel Cracker Candy (page 127), Spiced Pumpkin Snaps Dog Treats (page 119), and Cinnamon-Sugar Bourbon-Pumpkin Muffins (page 122).

And of course sweet bites—Cherry-White Chocolate Chip Cookies (page 96), and Fudge Ripple Pecan Brownies (page 114).

Happy Cooking! Happy Holidays!

TRES LECHES
BREAD PUDDING,
PAGE 84

MASHED ROOTS AND
POTATOES, PAGE 17

MUSHROOM GRAVY WITH
SHERRY AND THYME, PAGE 17

Holiday Dinner

Follow these recipes to serve a fabulous feast—from impressive main
dishes to stuffings and vegetable sides to round out your menu.

HERB-ROASTED
CHICKEN AND
VEGETABLES, PAGE 13

PEPPERCORN-CRUSTED HAM

PREP 15 minutes
ROAST 1 hour 20 minutes at 325°F
STAND 15 minutes

1 6- to 8-lb. cooked, bone-in spiral-sliced ham
1 12-oz. jar apricot preserves
¾ cup Dijon mustard
1 to 2 Tbsp. whole pink or mixed peppercorns
½ cup snipped dried apricots (optional)
   Halved apricots and Boston lettuce leaves (optional)

1. Preheat oven to 325°F. Place ham on wire rack in a shallow roasting pan. Tent with foil; crimp foil to pan edges. Roast 1 to 1¾ hours or until a thermometer registers 130°F.
2. Remove foil from ham. In a medium bowl stir together preserves and mustard; set aside ¾ cup. Brush remaining preserves mixture on top and sides of ham. Sprinkle with peppercorns. Cover cut side of ham with foil to prevent drying. Roast 20 to 30 minutes or until a thermometer registers 140°F. Remove from oven; remove foil. Let stand at least 15 minutes.
3. Meanwhile, for sauce, in a small saucepan combine reserved preserves mixture and snipped apricots, if using; heat through. Slice ham; serve warm or at room temperature with sauce. Garnish with apricots and lettuce if desired. Makes 16 servings.
PER SERVING *249 cal., 5 g fat (2 g sat. fat), 85 mg chol., 1,862 mg sodium, 19 g carb., 1 g fiber, 13 g sugars, 30 g pro.*

PAN-ROASTED BEEF TENDERLOIN WITH MUSHROOMS

PREP 25 minutes
STAND 30 minutes
ROAST 30 minutes at 425°F
COOK 20 minutes

1 2-lb. beef tenderloin, trimmed and tied
2 tsp. kosher salt
2 tsp. cracked black pepper
1 tsp. canola or corn oil
2 Tbsp. unsalted butter
2 Tbsp. extra-virgin olive oil
1 lb. cremini mushrooms or mixed cremini and shiitake, trimmed and sliced ¼ inch thick
⅓ cup finely chopped shallots
3 large cloves garlic, minced
⅓ cup dry sherry
1½ tsp. finely chopped fresh thyme

1. Position rack in center of oven. Preheat oven to 425°F. Pat beef dry. Let stand at room temperature 30 minutes. Season beef on all sides with kosher salt and cracked black pepper.
2. Heat canola oil in an extra-large ovenproof skillet over medium-high. Sear beef on all sides 8 to 10 minutes. Transfer skillet to oven. Roast 30 to 35 minutes or until a thermometer registers 135°F. Transfer beef to a platter; tent loosely with foil while preparing mushrooms.
3. Add 1 tablespoon butter and the olive oil to same skillet. Add mushrooms and a pinch of kosher salt. Cook over medium-high, stirring occasionally, until mushrooms begin to turn golden, 6 to 8 minutes. Add shallots; cook and stir 2 minutes. Add garlic; cook and stir 30 seconds. Season with additional salt and pepper. Carefully add sherry; cook and stir until almost evaporated, about 1 minute.
4. Stir juices from tenderloin platter into mushrooms with remaining butter and the thyme. Slice beef and serve with mushrooms. Makes 4 servings.
PER SERVING *506 cal., 27 g fat (9 g sat. fat), 154 mg chol., 757 mg sodium, 9 g carb., 2 g fiber, 4 g sugars, 54 g pro.*

PAN-ROASTED BEEF
TENDERLOIN WITH
MUSHROOMS

SPICED WINE-BRAISED
SHORT RIBS

SPICED WINE-BRAISED SHORT RIBS

PREP 40 minutes
BAKE 2 hours at 325°F plus 1 hour at 300°F

8   bone-in beef short ribs (about
    4 lb.), trimmed of fat
    Kosher salt
    Black pepper
3   Tbsp. canola or corn oil
1   large onion, chopped
2   medium carrots, chopped
½   of a fennel bulb, cored and
    chopped (about ½ cup)
3   garlic cloves, minced
1   Tbsp. tomato paste
2¼ cups dry red wine
1   cup reduced-sodium beef or
    chicken broth
½   of a small bunch fresh thyme
2   bay leaves
2   3-inch cinnamon sticks
8   whole peppercorns
5   whole cloves
3   whole allspice

1. Preheat oven to 325°F. Pat short ribs
dry; season generously with salt and
pepper. Heat 2 tablespoons oil in a
4- to 6-quart Dutch oven over medium-
high. Add half the ribs. Cook until well
browned on all sides, 3 to 4 minutes per
side. Transfer to a platter and repeat
with remaining ribs. Discard fat from pot.
2. Reduce heat to medium. Add the
remaining 1 tablespoon oil to pot. Add
onion, carrots, and fennel; cook and
stir 8 minutes or until softened. Add
garlic; cook and stir just until fragrant.
Add tomato paste; cook and stir
30 seconds. Carefully add ¼ cup wine;
cook until almost evaporated, scraping
up browned bits. Add remaining wine,
the broth, and thyme to pot; return
short ribs and juices from platter. Bring
to boiling.
3. Add bay leaves, cinnamon sticks,
peppercorns, cloves, and allspice. Cover
and transfer to oven. Bake 2 hours.
Reduce heat to 300°F; bake 1 hour more.
4. Transfer ribs to a baking dish; cool
slightly. Cool juices slightly; skim fat. Pour
sauce through a fine-mesh sieve; discard
solids. Place juices in a large pot. Bring to
boiling; reduce heat. Simmer, uncovered,
10 minutes. Add ribs and heat through
before serving. Makes 8 servings.
PER SERVING 506 cal., 28 g fat
(10 g sat. fat), 172 mg chol., 416 mg sodium,
7 g carb., 1 g fiber, 3 g sugars, 46 g pro.

HERB-ROASTED CHICKEN
AND VEGETABLES

HERB-ROASTED CHICKEN AND VEGETABLES

PREP 20 minutes
ROAST 1 hour 30 minutes at 375°F
STAND 10 minutes

1   4- to 5-lb. whole broiler-fryer
    chicken
2   Tbsp. butter, softened
2   cloves garlic, minced
1   tsp. dried basil, crushed
1   tsp. dried sage, crushed
½   tsp. dried thyme, crushed
½   tsp. salt
½   tsp. black pepper
1   lb. red-skin potatoes, cut into
    1-inch pieces
3   carrots, halved lengthwise and cut
    into 1-inch pieces
1   medium turnip, peeled and cut
    into 1½-inch pieces
1   medium onion, cut into 1-inch
    chunks
2   Tbsp. butter, melted
1   Tbsp. vegetable oil

1. Preheat oven to 375°F. Rinse chicken
body cavity; pat dry. Skewer neck skin
to back; tie legs to tail. Twist wing tips
under back. Place chicken, breast side
up, on a rack in a shallow roasting pan.
2. In a small bowl combine softened
butter and garlic; spread over chicken.
In another small bowl stir together basil,
sage, thyme, and ¼ teaspoon each salt
and pepper; sprinkle over chicken.
3. In a large bowl combine potatoes,
carrots, turnip, and onion; drizzle with
melted butter and oil. Sprinkle with
remaining salt and pepper; toss to coat.
Set aside.
4. Roast chicken 1 hour; cut string and
arrange vegetables around chicken
in pan. Roast 30 to 45 minutes more
or until chicken is done (170°F in thigh),
stirring vegetables once or twice.
Remove from oven. Cover and let
stand 10 minutes before carving. Makes
4 servings.
PER SERVING 897 cal., 60 g fat (21 g
sat. fat), 260 mg chol., 628 mg sodium,
27 g carb., 4 g fiber, 6 g sugars, 61 g pro.

THREE-CHEESE
PUMPKIN LASAGNA

THREE-CHEESE PUMPKIN LASAGNA

PREP 25 minutes
ROAST 25 minutes at 425°F
BAKE 55 minutes at 375°F
STAND 15 minutes

4	cups cubed fresh pumpkin or butternut squash (1¼ lb.)
8	oz. fresh cremini and/or button mushrooms, quartered
1	medium onion, cut into wedges
4	cloves garlic, peeled
2	10-oz. containers cherry tomatoes
¼	cup olive oil
½	tsp. salt
¼	tsp. black pepper
3	cups chopped fresh stemmed kale
1	Tbsp. chopped fresh sage
9	dried no-boil, oven-ready lasagna noodle sheets, such as Barilla
1	8-oz. container whipped cream cheese
1½	cups shredded mozzarella cheese (6 oz.)
6	Tbsp. grated Parmesan cheese
1½	cups vegetable broth

1. Preheat oven to 425°F. Place pumpkin, mushrooms, onion, and garlic in a 15×10-inch baking pan. Place tomatoes in another shallow baking pan. Drizzle each pan with 2 tablespoons oil and sprinkle with the salt and pepper; toss to coat. Spread in an even layer. Roast on separate oven racks 25 minutes or until pumpkin is tender, stirring twice and rotating baking pans once. Remove and stir pumpkin mixture and tomatoes together with liquid in an extra-large bowl. Add kale and sage and stir to combine. Reduce oven temperature to 375°F.

2. To assemble, spoon ½ cup of the vegetable mixture in a 13×9-inch baking dish. Top with 3 uncooked noodles. Top with one-third remaining vegetable mixture. Spoon mounds of one-third of the cream cheese over vegetables. Sprinkle with one-third of the mozzarella and 2 tablespoons Parmesan. Repeat layers twice. Pour vegetable broth over all. Cover; bake 40 minutes. Uncover; bake 15 to 20 minutes more or until noodles are tender. Remove and let stand 15 minutes before serving. Makes 8 servings.

PER SERVING *321 cal., 18 g fat (8 g sat. fat), 42 mg chol., 608 mg sodium, 31 g carb., 4 g fiber, 7 g sugars, 13 g pro.*

WILD MUSHROOM AND BLUE CHEESE BREAD PUDDING

PREP 25 minutes
SLOW COOK 5 hours (low)
STAND 15 minutes

5 cups 1-inch Italian flatbread (focaccia) cubes
1½ cups assorted chopped fresh wild mushrooms, such as chanterelle, morel, and/or stemmed shiitake
4 oz. smoked andouille sausage or other smoked sausage, chopped
½ cup chopped onion
½ cup crumbled blue cheese (2 oz.)
4 eggs, lightly beaten, or 1 cup refrigerated or frozen egg product, thawed
2 cups half-and-half, light cream, or milk
1 tsp. dried thyme, crushed
½ tsp. dried rosemary, crushed
½ tsp. black pepper

1. Line a 3½- or 4-quart slow cooker with a disposable slow cooker liner; set cooker aside. In a large bowl combine focaccia cubes, mushrooms, sausage, onion, and blue cheese. Transfer focaccia mixture to prepared cooker. In a medium bowl combine eggs, half-and-half, thyme, rosemary, and pepper. Pour over mixture in cooker.

2. Cover and cook on low 5 to 5½ hours. Turn off cooker. Let stand, covered, 15 to 30 minutes before serving. Makes 8 servings.

PER SERVING 233 cal., 13 g fat (7 g sat. fat), 140 mg chol., 357 mg sodium, 17 g carb., 1 g fiber, 1 g sugars, 12 g pro.

WILD MUSHROOM
AND BLUE CHEESE
BREAD PUDDING

WILD RICE STUFFING WITH
SQUASH AND MUSHROOMS

NO-BAKE HARVEST STUFFING

NO-BAKE HARVEST STUFFING

PREP 20 minutes
SLOW COOK 5 hours (low) or
2½ hours (high)

½   cup butter
1½ cups chopped onion
1½ cups chopped celery
4   cloves garlic, minced
¼   cup snipped fresh sage
½   tsp. salt
¼   tsp. black pepper
12 cups dry multigrain seeded
    sandwich bread cubes*
¾   cup dried cranberries
1   to 1½ cups turkey stock or
    reduced-sodium chicken broth
1   cup chopped toasted walnuts

1. In a large skillet melt butter over
medium heat. Add onion, celery, and
garlic; cook, stirring occasionally, until
tender, about 10 minutes. Remove from
heat. Stir in sage, salt, and pepper.
2. Place bread cubes and cranberries in
a 6-quart slow cooker. Add vegetable
mixture; stir to combine. Drizzle
with enough broth to moisten; toss
lightly to coat.
3. Cover and cook on low 5 to 6 hours
or high 2½ to 3 hours. Before serving,
gently stir in walnuts. Makes 10 servings.

*For Dry Bread Cubes Cut 18 to
21 slices fresh bread into ½-inch cubes.
Spread cubes in two 15×10-inch baking
pans. Bake 10 to 15 minutes at 300°F or
until dry, stirring twice; cool. (Bread will
continue to dry and crisp as it cools.)
Or, if time permits, let bread cubes sit
out, loosely covered, for 8 to 12 hours.
PER SERVING *353 cal., 18 g fat*
(6 g sat. fat), 24 mg chol., 516 mg sodium,
45 g carb., 4 g fiber, 8 g sugars, 8 g pro.

WILD RICE STUFFING WITH SQUASH AND MUSHROOMS

PREP 20 minutes
COOK 1 hour 15 minutes
BAKE 30 minutes at 375°F

3¼ cups chicken broth
1⅓ cups wild rice
¼   cup butter
1   cup chopped onion
½   cup chopped celery
2   tsp. poultry seasoning
8   oz. button mushrooms, thinly
    sliced (about 3 cups)
1   2-lb. butternut squash, seeded,
    peeled, and cut into ½-inch cubes
    (4 cups)

½   tsp. salt
¼   cup chopped fresh flat-leaf
    parsley

1. In a medium saucepan bring broth
to boiling over medium. Add wild
rice; reduce heat. Cover and simmer
50 minutes. Remove from heat; drain
if needed.
2. Preheat oven to 375°F. In a large
skillet melt 2 tablespoons butter over
medium. Add onion, celery, and
poultry seasoning; cook 4 minutes. Add
mushrooms; cook 4 minutes more or
until vegetables are tender. Remove to
a large bowl.
3. Add remaining butter to skillet. Add
squash cubes and salt; cook 15 minutes
or until nearly tender.
4. Add wild rice and squash to mixture
in bowl. Transfer to a buttered 3-quart
baking dish. Cover; bake 20 minutes.
Uncover; bake 10 minutes more or until
heated through. Top with parsley before
serving. Makes 8 servings.
PER SERVING *199 cal., 6 g fat (4 g sat. fat),*
17 mg chol., 553 mg sodium, 32 g carb.,
4 g fiber, 4 g sugars, 6 g pro.

MASHED ROOTS AND POTATOES

PREP 30 minutes
COOK 25 minutes

- 1 Tbsp. salt
- 1 1-lb. celery root, peeled and cut into ¾-inch chunks
- ¾ lb. parsnips, peeled and cut into ¾-inch chunks
- 1¼ lb. Yukon gold potatoes, peeled and cut into ¾-inch chunks
- 1 lb. russet potatoes, peeled and cut into ¾-inch chunks
- ¾ cup whole milk
- ¼ cup butter
- ⅔ cup sour cream
- 2 tsp. kosher salt
- ¼ tsp. ground white or black pepper
- ¼ tsp. freshly ground nutmeg

1. In a 6-quart pot bring 4 quarts water and 1 tablespoon salt to boiling. Add celery root and parsnips. Return to boiling; reduce heat. Cook, uncovered, 10 minutes. Add potatoes. Return to boiling; reduce heat and cook until potatoes and root vegetables are tender, 13 to 15 minutes more. Drain vegetables and return to pot. Set over low heat; toss vegetables to dry slightly.
2. While root vegetables and potato are cooking, heat milk and butter in small saucepan until butter is melted; set aside.
3. Mash potatoes and root vegetables until smooth. Add milk mixture to potatoes; stir to combine. Stir in sour cream, kosher salt, pepper, nutmeg, and additional milk as needed to reach desired consistency. Makes 8 servings.
PER SERVING 245 cal., 10 g fat (6 g sat. fat), 27 mg chol., 616 mg sodium, 36 g carb., 6 g fiber, 6 g sugars, 5 g pro.

MUSHROOM GRAVY WITH SHERRY AND THYME

MASHED ROOTS AND POTATOES

MUSHROOM GRAVY WITH SHERRY AND THYME

PREP 15 minutes
COOK 45 minutes

- 8 Tbsp. butter
- 1 medium onion, chopped
- 3 cloves garlic, finely chopped
- 1 Tbsp. tomato paste
- ⅔ cup dry sherry
- 4 cups vegetable broth
- ½ oz. dried porcini mushrooms (about ½ cup)
- 3 large thyme sprigs
- 6 Tbsp. all-purpose flour
  Freshly ground black pepper

1. In a medium saucepan melt 2 tablespoons butter over medium. Add onion; cook, stirring occasionally, until softened but not browned, about 5 minutes. Add garlic; cook 1 minute more. Add tomato paste; cook, stirring until color deepens, about 2 minutes. Add sherry; bring to a boil. Reduce heat and simmer until reduced slightly, about 3 minutes. Add broth, dried mushrooms, and thyme sprigs; bring to a boil. Simmer 30 minutes. Strain through a fine-mesh sieve into a bowl, pressing on solids (discard solids). Do not wash pan.
2. Melt remaining 6 tablespoons butter in the same saucepan over medium. Add flour; cook, whisking, 1 to 2 minutes (do not let flour brown). Add about ½ cup of the hot broth, whisking to blend. Add remaining broth a little at a time, whisking until gravy is smooth. Season with pepper. Makes 12 servings.
PER SERVING 111 cal., 8 g fat (5 g sat. fat), 20 mg chol., 339 mg sodium, 6 g carb., 0 g fiber, 2 g sugars, 1 g pro.

**ROASTED POTATOES,
FENNEL, AND LEMON**

PARMESAN-ROASTED
CAULIFLOWER

PREP 15 minutes
ROAST 23 minutes at 450°F

6   cups cauliflower florets
1   Tbsp. olive oil
     Salt and black pepper
½   cup shredded Parmesan cheese
     (2 oz.)
¼   cup butter
2   cloves garlic, minced
⅔   cup slivered almonds, chopped
⅔   cup panko bread crumbs

1. Preheat oven to 450°F. Place
cauliflower in a 15×10-inch baking pan.
Drizzle with oil and sprinkle with salt and
pepper; toss to coat. Roast 20 minutes.
Stir in cheese. Roast 3 to 5 minutes more
or until cauliflower is crisp-tender.
2. Meanwhile, in a medium skillet melt
butter over medium. Add garlic; cook
and stir 20 seconds. Stir in almonds
and panko. Cook over medium-low
to medium until golden. Sprinkle
cauliflower with almond mixture. Makes
8 servings.
PER SERVING 175 cal., 14 g fat (5 g sat. fat),
19 mg chol., 319 mg sodium, 9 g carb.,
3 g fiber, 2 g sugars, 6 g pro.

ROASTED POTATOES,
FENNEL, AND LEMON

PREP 15 minutes
ROAST 40 minutes at 450°F

1½ lb. red and yellow fingerling
     potatoes, halved or quartered
     lengthwise
1   bulb fennel, ends trimmed, cut into
     8 wedges
2   shallots, cut into wedges
1   lemon, quartered
2   Tbsp. extra-virgin olive oil
½   tsp. salt
¼   tsp. black pepper

1. Preheat oven to 450°F. In a 15×10-inch
baking pan combine potatoes, fennel,
shallots, and lemon. Drizzle with olive
oil. Sprinkle with the salt and pepper.
Toss to coat; spread in pan in a
single layer.
3. Roast, uncovered, until tender
and browned, stirring twice, about
40 minutes. Makes 4 servings.
PER SERVING 210 cal., 7 g fat (1 g sat. fat),
0 mg chol., 354 mg sodium, 36 g carb.,
6 g fiber, 6 g sugars, 5 g pro.

ROASTED BROCCOLI WITH PECORINO AND LEMON

PREP 15 minutes
ROAST 25 minutes at 425°F

- 1¼ lb. broccoli florets, halved if large
- ¼ cup extra-virgin olive oil
- ¾ tsp. kosher salt
- ¼ tsp. black pepper
- 1 lemon
- 1 oz. Pecorino Romano cheese or Parmesan cheese, finely shredded

1. Preheat oven to 425°F. Line a 15×10-inch baking pan with foil. Add broccoli and olive oil to the pan; toss to coat, arranging large pieces near edges of pan. Season with salt and pepper. Roast 15 minutes. Rotate pan and roast just until broccoli is tender and charred, about 10 minutes more.
2. Zest lemon over broccoli; squeeze juice from half the lemon over the broccoli. Sprinkle with cheese. Makes 4 servings.
PER SERVING *197 cal., 16 g fat (3 g sat. fat), 7 mg chol., 359 mg sodium, 10 g carb., 4 g fiber, 3 g sugars, 6 g pro.*

ROASTED BROCCOLI WITH PECORINO AND LEMON

GREEN BEAN CASSEROLE

GREEN BEAN CASSEROLE

PREP 25 minutes
COOK 30 minutes
BAKE 25 minutes at 375°F

½   cup canola or corn oil
4   large shallots, 3 thinly sliced
     (about 1 cup) and 1 finely chopped
     (⅓ cup)
4   tsp. cornstarch
1½   lb. green beans, trimmed and
     halved crosswise
3   Tbsp. butter
1   lb. cremini mushrooms, roughly
     chopped
2   large cloves garlic, finely chopped
¼   cup Madeira wine or chicken broth
2½   Tbsp. all-purpose flour
1¼   cups reduced-sodium chicken
     broth
⅔   cup heavy cream
½   tsp. kosher salt
½   tsp. black pepper
¼   tsp. freshly ground nutmeg

1. In a medium skillet heat oil until shimmering. Separate sliced shallots into rings; toss in a small bowl with cornstarch. Shake off excess in a fine-mesh strainer. Add one-fourth of the shallots to pan. Cook, tossing frequently, until lightly golden, about 4 minutes. Using a slotted spoon, transfer shallots to a plate lined with paper towels. Repeat with remaining sliced shallots.
2. Bring a large saucepan of salted water to a boil; prepare an ice bath. Cook beans in water 4 minutes or just until crisp-tender. Transfer to ice bath; drain and pat dry.
3. Preheat oven to 375°F. In an extra-large skillet melt butter over medium-high. Add mushrooms. Cook, tossing occasionally, until mushrooms release their liquid, about 5 minutes.

Add chopped shallots and garlic; cook, stirring, 2 minutes. Add Madeira; cook, stirring, until almost evaporated. Add flour; stir to coat mushrooms; cook 1 minute. Add about half the broth, scraping up bits from bottom of pan. Add remaining broth and cream; bring to a simmer. Cook until thickened slightly, about 5 minutes. Season with kosher salt, pepper, and nutmeg. Add green beans; stir to coat.
4. Transfer mixture to a 3-quart baking dish (or bake in skillet, if oven-proof). Bake, uncovered, until bubbling around edges, about 25 minutes. Sprinkle fried shallots on casserole. Makes 8 servings.
Make Ahead Assemble casserole (minus the topping) 1 day ahead. Cover and refrigerate. Bring to room temperature before baking.
PER SERVING *303 cal., 25 g fat (9 g sat. fat), 34 mg chol., 207 mg sodium, 15 g carb., 3 g fiber, 6 g sugars, 5 g pro.*

ROASTED CARROTS WITH LEMON-CUMIN AÏOLI

PREP 15 minutes
ROAST 25 minutes at 425°F

1½ lb. carrots, peeled and bias-sliced ¼ inch thick
2 Tbsp. plus 1 tsp. extra-virgin olive oil
   Kosher salt
   Black pepper
1⅛ tsp. honey
¼ cup raw pumpkin seeds (pepitas)
¼ tsp. plus a generous pinch ground cumin
¼ cup mayonnaise
½ tsp. lemon zest
1 tsp. fresh lemon juice
½ of a small clove garlic, minced

1. For carrots, preheat oven to 425°F. Pile carrots in center of a large rimmed baking sheet. Drizzle with 2 tablespoons oil and sprinkle generously with salt and pepper. Toss with hands to coat, then spread evenly. Cover pan tightly with foil. Roast 10 minutes. Remove foil, drizzle carrots with 1 teaspoon honey, then toss to coat. Continue roasting, uncovered, until carrots are tender and lightly charred, about 15 minutes. (Carrots can be roasted a few hours ahead and set aside.)

2. In a small oven-proof skillet toss pumpkin seeds with remaining 1 teaspoon oil. Season with a pinch each of cumin, salt, and pepper; toss to coat. To toast seeds, put in oven with carrots during the last 10 minutes of roasting time. Transfer to a plate lined with paper towels; cool.

3. For aïoli, in a small bowl combine mayonnaise, lemon zest and juice, garlic, remaining ¼ teaspoon cumin, and remaining ⅛ teaspoon honey. Season with pepper. (Aïoli can be made 1 day ahead and refrigerated in an airtight container.)

4. To serve, arrange carrots on a platter, drizzle with aïoli, and sprinkle with pumpkin seeds. Makes 8 servings.

PER SERVING 141 cal., 11 g fat (2 g sat. fat), 3 mg chol., 182 mg sodium, 9 g carb., 2 g fiber, 5 g sugars, 2 g pro.

ROASTED CARROTS WITH LEMON-CUMIN AÏOLI

WINTER TABBOULEH WITH FENNEL AND CRANBERRIES

KALE, FENNEL, AND ROASTED DELICATA SALAD WITH MISO-LEMON VINAIGRETTE

PREP 15 minutes
ROAST 20 minutes at 450°F plus 5 minutes at 400°F

1   lb. delicata squash, halved lengthwise, seeded (reserve seeds), and cut into 1-inch pieces.
¼   cup plus 4 tsp. olive oil
½   tsp. salt
¼   tsp. freshly ground black pepper
¼   cup golden raisins
1   Tbsp. sherry vinegar
2   Tbsp. lemon juice
1   Tbsp. white miso paste
1   small garlic clove, minced
6   cups stemmed and torn kale
1   cup quartered and thinly sliced fennel

1. Preheat oven to 450°F. Place squash in a 15×10-inch baking pan. Drizzle with 3 teaspoons oil; sprinkle with salt and pepper. Roast 10 minutes. Turn squash; roast 10 minutes more or until browned and tender.
2. Meanwhile, rinse squash seeds in a small bowl of cold water to remove any pulp. Spread on paper towels to dry.
3. In the same bowl combine raisins, vinegar, and 1 tablespoon water. Microwave 1 minute or until bubbly; cool.
4. When squash is done, remove from pan. Reduce oven temperature to 400°F. In another small bowl combine squash seeds and 1 teaspoon oil; toss to coat. Sprinkle with additional salt and pepper. Spread seeds in baking pan and roast 5 minutes or until toasted.
5. In a large bowl whisk together lemon juice, miso paste, and garlic until smooth. Slowly add ¼ cup oil, whisking until combined. Add kale; toss until coated then gently massage leaves. Add fennel and roasted squash; toss to combine. Top salad with raisins with liquid and toasted seeds. Makes 4 servings.
PER SERVING *285 cal., 19 g fat (3 g sat. fat), 0 mg chol., 538 mg sodium, 26 g carb., 6 g fiber, 15 g sugars, 7 g pro.*

WINTER TABBOULEH WITH FENNEL AND CRANBERRIES

PREP 20 minutes
COOK 20 minutes

½   cup quinoa
¼   cup fresh lemon juice
¼   cup extra-virgin olive oil
1   garlic clove, minced
1   tsp. dried mint
½   tsp. kosher salt
¼   tsp. ground allspice
¼   tsp. black pepper
2   large bunches flat-leaf parsley, finely chopped (about 4 packed cups)
½   of a medium fennel bulb, finely diced (about 1 cup)
4   green onions, thinly sliced
¼   cup dried cranberries, coarsely chopped
¼   cup roasted sunflower seeds

1. Rinse quinoa well in a fine-mesh sieve. Add to a medium saucepan; cook and stir over medium until dry and lightly toasted, about 5 minutes. Add 1 cup water; bring to a boil. Reduce heat to medium-low; simmer, covered, until quinoa is tender, about 15 minutes. Spread onto a baking sheet to cool.
2. In a medium serving bowl whisk together lemon juice, oil, garlic, mint, salt, allspice, and pepper.
3. Add parsley, fennel, green onions, and cooled quinoa to bowl; toss well. Fold in cranberries and sunflower seeds; season with additional salt. Makes 6 servings.
PER SERVING *202 cal., 13 g fat (2 g sat. fat), 0 mg chol., 494 mg sodium, 19 g carb., 4 g fiber, 5 g sugars, 5 g pro.*

KALE, FENNEL, AND ROASTED DELICATA SALAD WITH MISO-LEMON VINAIGRETTE

CURRIED CELERY SOUP WITH PEAR

PREP 20 minutes
COOK 20 minutes

2   Tbsp. olive oil
1   medium onion, chopped
1   tsp. curry powder
1   tsp. dried rosemary, crushed
1   lb. bunch celery, chopped (about 4 cups), leaves removed
3½ cups reduced-sodium chicken broth
¼   cup uncooked long or medium grain white rice
    Pear slices

1. In a medium saucepan heat oil over medium. Add onion; cook 3 minutes or until transparent. Add curry powder and rosemary; cook and stir 30 seconds more.
2. Add celery, broth, and rice. Bring to boiling; reduce heat, cover, and simmer 20 minutes or until celery and rice are very tender. Cool slightly.
3. Transfer to a blender or food processor in batches; cover and blend or process until smooth. (Or use an immersion blender in the pot.)
4. To serve, top soup with pear slices and celery leaves. Makes 4 servings.
PER SERVING *155 cal., 7 g fat (1 g sat. fat), 0 mg chol., 568 mg sodium, 19 g carb., 3 g fiber, 5 g sugars, 5 g pro.*

RED CABBAGE AND RADICCHIO SLAW

PREP 20 minutes
CHILL 1 hour

⅓   cup olive oil
3   Tbsp. red wine vinegar
2   Tbsp. finely chopped red onion
1   Tbsp. sugar
2   tsp. fennel seeds, lightly crushed
1   tsp. salt
½   tsp. cracked black pepper
3   cups shredded red cabbage
2   cups shredded radicchio
¼   cup pomegranate seeds

1. In a medium bowl whisk together olive oil, vinegar, red onion, sugar, fennel seeds, salt, and pepper. Add cabbage and radicchio; toss to coat. Cover and chill at least 1 hour or up to 4 hours.
2. To serve, top slaw with pomegranate seeds. Makes 6 servings.
PER SERVING *140 cal., 12 g fat (2 g sat. fat), 0 mg chol., 387 mg sodium, 7 g carb., 2 g fiber, 5 g sugars, 1 g pro.*

GINGER-CRANBERRY RELISH

PREP 20 minutes
CHILL 1 hour

1   large orange
1   12-oz. pkg. fresh or frozen cranberries, thawed if frozen (3 cups)
1   small red apple, cored and coarsely chopped
½   tsp. kosher salt
⅛   tsp. ground cloves
⅓   cup chopped walnuts, toasted*
¼   to ½ cup honey
3   Tbsp. finely chopped crystallized ginger

1. Using a vegetable peeler, remove three wide strips of zest from orange. If necessary, use a spoon to scrape any white pith off strips. Coarsely chop zest; you should have 1 tablespoon. Squeeze ⅓ cup juice from orange.
2. In a food processor combine zest, cranberries, apple, salt, and cloves; pulse until chopped. Add orange juice. Pulse three times or just until combined.
3. Transfer cranberry mixture to a medium bowl. Stir in walnuts, honey, and ginger. Chill, covered, at least 1 hour or up to 1 day. If desired, top with additional toasted walnuts. Makes 6 servings.
*Tip To toast nuts, preheat oven to 350°F. Spread nuts in a shallow baking pan. Bake 5 to 10 minutes or until nuts are light brown, shaking pan once or twice.
PER SERVING *84 cal., 4 g fat (0 g sat. fat), 0 mg chol., 95 mg sodium, 11 g carb., 2 g fiber, 5 g sugars, 1 g pro.*

CURRIED CELERY SOUP WITH PEAR

GINGER-CRANBERRY
RELISH

RED CABBAGE AND
RADICCHIO SLAW

TWICE-BAKED
POTATO BITES, PAGE 30

Festive Appetizers

A selection of savory appetizers is the best kind of party food.

These dips, mushrooms, wings, and other nibbles are terrific alone

as starters or as part of an appetizer buffet.

CHEESE FONDUE,
PAGE 36

BACON-FILLED MEDJOOL DATES

PREP 25 minutes
BAKE 12 minutes at 375°F

6   slices bacon
½   cup whole almonds or pecan halves, toasted and chopped (tip, page 24)
½   cup finely shredded Manchego or Parmesan cheese (2 oz.)
24 unpitted whole Medjool dates (about 1 lb.)
3   Tbsp. honey
1   tsp. snipped fresh thyme

1. Preheat oven to 375°F. In a large skillet cook bacon over medium until crisp. Transfer bacon to paper towels to drain; crumble bacon. In a bowl stir together the bacon, almonds, and cheese.
2. Cut a slit along one side of each date and remove pit. Spoon about 1 tablespoon filling into each date; press date to shape around filling (filling will be exposed). Arrange dates, filling sides up, in an ungreased 13×9-inch baking pan.
3. Bake 12 to 15 minutes or until heated through and cheese is lightly browned; cool slightly. Before serving, drizzle warm dates with honey and sprinkle with thyme. Makes 24 servings.
Make Ahead Prepare as directed through Step 2. Cover and refrigerate up to 2 days. Continue as directed, baking 15 to 18 minutes.
PER SERVING *112 cal., 3 g fat (1 g sat. fat), 4 mg chol., 79 mg sodium, 21 g carb., 2 g fiber, 18 g sugars, 2 g pro.*

HERB- AND- GOAT-CHEESE-STUFFED MUSHROOMS

PREP 40 minutes
BAKE 15 minutes at 400°F

24 large fresh cremini mushrooms, about 1½ inches in diameter
2   Tbsp. olive oil
¾   tsp. salt
1   Tbsp. butter
1   Tbsp. finely chopped shallot
3   cloves garlic, minced
1   tsp. snipped fresh thyme
¼   cup dry sherry
¾   cup panko
2   Tbsp. snipped fresh chives

HERB- AND- GOAT- CHEESE-STUFFED MUSHROOMS

2   tsp. lemon zest
1   cup crumbled chèvre (4 oz.)
¼   cup pine nuts, toasted (tip, page 24)
    Snipped fresh chives (optional)

1. Remove stems from mushrooms; chop stems and set aside. In a small bowl combine 1 tablespoon of the oil and ¼ teaspoon of the salt; brush mixture onto mushroom caps.
2. For filling, in a large skillet heat the remaining 1 tablespoon oil and the butter over medium-high. Add mushroom stems, shallot, garlic, thyme, and the remaining ½ teaspoon salt. Cook and stir 8 to 10 minutes or until stems are tender and liquid is evaporated. Remove from heat; carefully add sherry. Return to heat; cook until sherry is evaporated, stirring to scrape up any crusty browned bits. Cool 10 minutes. Stir in panko, 2 tablespoons chives, and lemon zest. Stir in goat cheese and pine nuts.
3. Preheat oven to 400°F. Line a 15×10-inch baking pan with parchment paper. Arrange mushroom caps, stemmed sides up, in prepared pan. Generously fill mushrooms with filling.
4. Bake, uncovered, 15 minutes or until mushrooms are tender and filling is bubbly around the edges. If desired, sprinkle with additional chives. Serve warm. Makes 24 servings.
PER SERVING *56 cal., 4 g fat (2 g sat. fat), 5 mg chol., 108 mg sodium, 3 g carb., 0 g fiber, 1 g sugars, 2 g pro.*

TWICE-BAKED POTATO BITES

melon baller or small spoon, scoop out potato flesh, leaving a ⅛-inch shell; transfer flesh to a large bowl. Mash potato flesh in bowl until smooth. Stir in two-thirds of the chopped bacon, the yogurt, cheeses, 1 tablespoon basil, the bell pepper, butter, and black pepper. Spoon or pipe potato mixture into prepared shells. Return filled potatoes to the baking pan. Bake 20 minutes or until potatoes and filling are heated through (165°F).

5. Sprinkle with basil leaves. Serve warm. Makes 14 servings.

PER SERVING 123 cal., 5 g fat (2 g sat. fat), 12 mg chol., 166 mg sodium, 15 g carb., 2 g fiber, 2 g sugars, 5 g pro.

PESTO ROLL-UPS

PREP 20 minutes
RISE 30 minutes
BAKE 20 minutes at 375°F

    Nonstick cooking spray
1   16-oz. loaf frozen whole wheat bread dough, thawed
⅓   cup purchased basil pesto
⅓   cup bottled roasted red bell peppers, drained, patted dry, and chopped
⅓   cup plus 1 Tbsp. finely shredded Parmesan cheese

1. Coat a 13×9-inch baking pan with cooking spray. On a lightly floured surface, roll bread dough into a 12×8-inch rectangle. Spread pesto over dough to within 1 inch of long sides. Sprinkle roasted peppers and ⅓ cup of the cheese over pesto. Starting from a long side, roll up rectangle into a spiral. Pinch dough to seal seams. Slice roll into 12 pieces. Arrange pieces in prepared pan. Cover; let rolls rise in a warm place until nearly double in size (30 to 45 minutes).

2. Preheat oven to 375°F. Uncover rolls and sprinkle with remaining 1 tablespoon cheese. Bake 20 to 25 minutes or until golden brown. Immediately remove rolls from pan; serve warm. Makes 12 servings.

PER SERVING 137 cal., 5 g fat (1 g sat. fat), 2 mg chol., 337 mg sodium, 19 g carb., 2 g fiber, 0 g sugars, 6 g pro.

TWICE-BAKED POTATO BITES

PREP 35 minutes
COOL 30 minutes
BAKE 35 minutes at 400°F plus 20 minutes at 350°F

14 2-inch round red potatoes
1   Tbsp. olive oil
⅛   tsp. salt
6   slices bacon
2   tsp. bottled barbecue sauce
½   cup plain full-fat Greek yogurt
½   cup shredded white cheddar cheese
⅓   cup shredded Parmesan cheese
1   Tbsp. finely snipped fresh basil
4   tsp. very finely chopped red bell pepper
2   tsp. butter, softened
    Pinch black pepper
    Small fresh basil leaves

1. Preheat oven to 400°F. Line a 15×10-inch baking pan with parchment paper. Place potatoes on prepared pan. Pierce potatoes with a fork. Drizzle with oil and season with salt. Bake 35 minutes or until tender when pricked with a fork. Let cool 30 minutes. Reduce oven temperature to 350°F.

2. Meanwhile, in a large nonstick skillet cook bacon over medium heat until crisp. Drain on paper towels. Drain and discard fat from skillet. Carefully wipe skillet clean with paper towels.

3. Return bacon to skillet over low heat. Brush bacon evenly with barbecue sauce. Cook, turning occasionally, 2 minutes or until glazed. Cool completely; finely chop bacon.

4. With a serrated knife cut a thin layer off the top of a potato. Using a

PESTO ROLL-UPS

ROSEMARY-ORANGE
MARINATED OLIVES

ROSEMARY-ORANGE MARINATED OLIVES

PREP 15 minutes
CHILL 24 hours
STAND 1 hour

2 cups Kalamata olives
3 sprigs fresh rosemary
¼ cup extra virgin olive oil
2 large cloves garlic, lightly crushed
2 wide strips orange zest, sliced in thin julienne pieces
½ tsp. fennel seeds, toasted* and crushed

1. Rinse olives and pat dry; place in a medium bowl. Add 2 rosemary sprigs and remaining ingredients; toss together. Cover and chill 24 to 48 hours, tossing once or twice.
2. Let stand at room temperature 1 hour before serving. Transfer to a serving bowl; replace rosemary sprigs with remaining fresh sprig. Makes 10 servings.
*Tip In a dry skillet toast seeds over medium heat 3 to 5 minutes, stirring frequently.
PER SERVING 94 cal., 10 g fat (1 g sat. fat), 0 mg chol., 420 mg sodium, 0 g carb., 0 g fiber, 0 g sugars, 0 g pro.

JALAPEÑO POPPER DEVILED EGGS

PREP 20 minutes
BAKE 7 minutes
STAND 1 minute

½ cup shredded pepper Jack cheese
12 hard-cooked eggs
3 Tbsp. mayonnaise
3 Tbsp. cream cheese, softened
1 jalapeño, seeded and finely chopped*
3 Tbsp. sliced green onions
    Salt and black pepper
3 slices bacon, crisp-cooked and finely crumbled
    Chili powder

1. Preheat oven to 400°F. Line a baking sheet with parchment paper. Place about 1 tablespoon of the shredded cheese on prepared sheet; pat into a 2-inch circle. Repeat with remaining cheese, allowing 2 inches between circles. Bake 7 to 8 minutes or until bubbly and lightly golden. Let stand on baking sheet 1 to 2 minutes or until cooled but still pliable. Carefully peel off paper. Place cheese crisps on a wire

JALAPEÑO POPPER DEVILED EGGS

rack; cool completely. Once cool, break cheese crisps into pieces.
2. Halve hard-cooked eggs lengthwise and remove yolks. Set whites aside. Place yolks in a small bowl; mash with a fork. Add mayonnaise, cream cheese, jalapeño, and green onions; mix well. Season to taste with salt and pepper. Fill egg halves with yolk filling and top each egg half with a bit of crispy cheese and bacon. Sprinkle with chili powder. Makes 24 servings.
*Tip Chile peppers contain oils that can irritate skin and eyes. Wear plastic or rubber gloves when working with them.
PER SERVING 68 cal., 5 g fat (2 g sat. fat), 99 mg chol., 108 mg sodium, 0 g carb., 0 g fiber, 0 g sugars, 4 g pro.

ROASTED SHRIMP COCKTAIL WITH BLOODY MARY SAUCE AND LEMON-CHIVE MAYO

PREP 20 minutes
STAND 10 minutes
ROAST 5 minutes at 400°F

2	lb. fresh or frozen (thawed) jumbo shrimp (21 to 25 per pound)
2	Tbsp. lemon juice
2	Tbsp. olive oil
½	tsp. kosher salt
	Lemon wedges
⅓	cup ketchup
⅓	cup bottled chili sauce
1	Tbsp. prepared horseradish
1	Tbsp. vodka
2	tsp. lemon juice
1	tsp. Worcestershire sauce
½	tsp. bottled hot pepper sauce
⅛	tsp. celery salt
	Freshly ground black pepper
½	cup mayonnaise
¼	cup snipped fresh chives
1	tsp. lemon zest
2	tsp. lemon juice
1	small clove garlic, pressed or minced
¼	tsp. sugar

1. For Roasted Shrimp, peel and devein shrimp, leaving tails intact. Preheat oven to 400°F. In a large bowl combine lemon juice, olive oil, and kosher salt. Add shrimp; toss. Let stand 10 minutes, tossing once or twice. Transfer shrimp to a 15×10-inch baking pan and spread evenly. Roast just until shrimp are pink and cooked through, about 5 minutes. Cool to room temperature; cover and refrigerate overnight or until well chilled. Serve with lemon wedges and sauces.
2. For Bloody Mary Cocktail Sauce, in a small bowl combine ketchup, chili sauce, vodka, horseradish, lemon juice, Worcestershire sauce, hot sauce, celery salt, and freshly ground black pepper to taste. Chill until ready to serve.
3. For Lemon-Chive Mayo, in a small bowl combine mayonnaise, chives, lemon zest, lemon juice, garlic, and sugar; season with kosher salt and freshly ground black pepper. Chill until ready to serve. Makes 8 servings.
PER SERVING *251 cal., 14 g fat (2 g sat. fat), 188 mg chol., 605 mg sodium, 7 g carb., 0 g fiber, 5 g sugars, 23 g pro.*

ROASTED SHRIMP COCKTAIL WITH BLOODY MARY COCKTAIL SAUCE AND LEMON-CHIVE MAYO

THAI CHICKEN WINGS WITH PEANUT SAUCE

PREP 25 minutes
SLOW COOK 5 hours (low) or
2½ hours (high)

- 24 chicken wing drummettes (about 2¼ lb. total)
- ½ cup salsa
- 2 Tbsp. creamy peanut butter
- 1 Tbsp. lime juice
- 2 tsp. soy sauce
- 2 tsp. grated fresh ginger
- ¼ cup sugar
- ¼ cup creamy peanut butter
- 3 Tbsp. soy sauce
- 3 Tbsp. water
- 2 cloves garlic, minced

1. Place chicken drummettes in a 3½- or 4-quart slow cooker. In a small bowl combine salsa, 2 tablespoons peanut butter, lime juice, 2 teaspoons soy sauce, and ginger. Pour salsa mixture over chicken; toss to coat.
2. Cover and cook on low 5 to 6 hours or high 2½ to 3 hours.
3. Meanwhile, for Peanut Sauce, in a small saucepan combine sugar, ¼ cup peanut butter, 3 tablespoons soy sauce, the water, and garlic. Cook and stir over medium-low until sugar is dissolved and mixture is smooth. Sauce will thicken as it cools.
4. Drain chicken, discarding cooking liquid. Return chicken to cooker. Gently stir in Peanut Sauce. Serve immediately or keep warm, covered, on warm or low-heat setting up to 2 hours. Makes 12 servings.
PER SERVING *189 cal., 13 g fat (3 g sat. fat), 58 mg chol., 392 mg sodium, 6 g carb., 1 g fiber, 5 g sugars, 12 g pro.*

ROASTED RED PEPPER-PECAN DIP

PREP 10 minutes
BROIL 8 minutes
STAND 1 hour 20 minutes

- 3 medium red bell peppers
- 1½ cups pecans, toasted (tip, page 24)
- ½ cup fresh bread crumbs
- 1 lemon, juiced (about 3 Tbsp.)
- 2 Tbsp. extra virgin olive oil
- 1 clove garlic
- 1 Tbsp. honey
- 1 tsp. ground cumin
- 1 tsp. salt
  Pinch cayenne pepper
  Crudités and cut-up vegetables

1. Position oven rack 4 to 6 inches from the broiler. Preheat broiler. Place peppers on a baking sheet; place sheet under broiler. Broil until charred, turning to char all sides., 8 to 10 minutes. Place peppers in a heat-proof bowl; cover and let stand 20 minutes. Remove stems, skins and seeds.
2. In a food processor combine roasted peppers, pecans, bread crumbs, lemon juice, olive oil, garlic, honey, cumin, salt, and cayenne pepper. Pulse until smooth. Cover; let stand 1 hour for flavors to blend. Drizzle with additional olive oil. Serve with crudités and vegetables. Makes 10 servings.
PER SERVING *152 cal., 14 g fat (1 g sat. fat), 0 mg chol., 246 mg sodium, 8 g carb., 2 g fiber, 4 g sugars, 2 g pro.*

ROASTED RED PEPPER-PECAN DIP

THAI CHICKEN WINGS WITH PEANUT SAUCE

CHEESE FONDUE

CHEESE FONDUE

START TO FINISH 20 minutes

1   lb. freshly shredded Gruyère cheese
1   Tbsp. cornstarch
1   cup dry unoaked white wine
1   tsp. minced garlic
    Assorted dippers such as dry sourdough or pumpernickel bread, dry smoked sausage or pan-fried smoked sausage, sliced pears or apples, roasted beets or steamed Brussels sprouts

1. In a large bowl toss the cheese with cornstarch until evenly coated.
2. In a medium saucepan bring the wine and garlic to a simmer over medium. About one-fourth at a time, stir cheese into wine mixture in saucepan. Return to a gentle simmer between additions. Stir until completely melted and smooth.
3. Transfer melted cheese to a fondue pot; serve immediately. (Or use a double boiler or small slow cooker set on warm.) Makes 8 servings.
PER SERVING *259 cal., 18 g fat (11 g sat. fat), 60 mg chol., 378 mg sodium, 2 g carb., 0 g fiber, 0 g sugars, 17 g pro.*

LEMON-DILL ARTICHOKE DIP

PREP 25 minutes
BAKE 25 minutes at 350°F
COOL 15 minutes

2   14-oz. cans artichoke hearts, rinsed and drained
1   medium fennel bulb, trimmed (reserve fronds if desired)
1   8-oz. carton sour cream
2   Tbsp. all-purpose flour
¾   cup finely shredded Parmesan cheese (3 oz.)
½   cup mayonnaise
¼   cup crumbled feta cheese (1 oz.)
¼   cup finely chopped red bell pepper
¼   cup chopped fresh dill
1   Tbsp. lemon zest
    Lemon slices (optional)

1. Preheat oven to 350°F. Place artichokes in a fine-mesh sieve. Press with paper towels to remove excess liquid. Chop artichokes. Quarter and core fennel; cut lengthwise into thin slices.

LEMON-DILL ARTICHOKE DIP

2. In a large bowl stir together sour cream and flour. Stir in artichokes, fennel, ½ cup Parmesan cheese, the mayonnaise, feta cheese, bell pepper, dill, and lemon zest. Transfer to a 9-inch cast-iron skillet. Sprinkle with remaining ¼ cup Parmesan cheese.

3. Bake 25 minutes or until center is bubbly and edges are lightly browned. Cool on a wire rack 15 minutes. If desired, top with lemon slices, fennel fronds, and/or additional feta cheese or dill. Makes 16 servings.

PER SERVING *112 cal., 9 g fat (3 g sat. fat), 17 mg chol., 222 mg sodium, 5 g carb., 1 g fiber, 2 g sugars, 2 g pro.*

PIZZA SUPREME DIP

START TO FINISH 35 minutes

8   oz. bulk Italian sausage
½   cup chopped onion
1   clove garlic, minced
1   15-oz. can pizza sauce
1   cup thinly sliced cooked turkey pepperoni or mini pepperoni, or chopped Canadian-style bacon
1   cup coarsely chopped fresh portobello or cremini mushrooms
½   cup coarsely chopped green bell pepper
¼   cup sliced pitted ripe olives
¾   cup shredded four-cheese pizza cheese (3 oz.)
1   recipe Pizza Chips, bagel chips, and/or toasted baguette-style French bread slices

1. Preheat broiler. In a seasoned or generously greased 8- to 9-inch cast-iron or oven-going skillet cook sausage, onion, and garlic over medium-high until sausage is browned. Drain off fat.

2. Stir in pizza sauce, pepperoni, mushrooms, bell pepper, and olives. Cook over medium heat until bubbly, stirring occasionally. Top with cheese.

3. Broil 3 to 4 inches from heat 2 to 3 minutes or just until cheese starts to brown. Serve with Pizza Chips. Makes 16 servings.

Slow Cooker Directions Prepare as directed in Step 1, using any medium skillet to cook sausage mixture. Stir in pizza sauce, pepperoni, mushrooms, bellpepper, and olives. Transfer dip to a 1½-quart slow cooker. Sprinkle with cheese. Cover and cook on low 4 hours or high 2 hours or until bubbly. Serve with Pizza Chips.

Pizza Chips Preheat broiler. Stack four 8-inch pizza crusts (such as Boboli). Cut through stack into eight wedges. Arrange wedges in a single layer on an extra-large baking sheet. Broil 4 inches from heat 4 minutes or until wedges are lightly toasted, turning once. Cool. Makes 32 chips.

PER SERVING *104 cal., 7 g fat (3 g sat. fat), 24 mg chol., 337 mg sodium, 4 g carb., 1 g fiber, 1 g sugars, 6 g pro.*

PIZZA SUPREME DIP

**CHEESY
ROSEMARY AND
PECAN SNACK MIX**

1. In a large pitcher combine orange sherbet, grenadine, and orange juice. Mash with a potato masher or wooden spoon until combined. Add ginger ale; stir to combine. Pour into ice-filled cocktail glasses. Makes 8 servings.
PER SERVING *184 cal., 1 g fat (0 g sat. fat), 0 mg chol., 35 mg sodium, 44 g carb., 1 g fiber, 37 g sugars, 1 g pro.*

EARL GREY HOT BUTTERED RUM

START TO FINISH 10 minutes

½	cup boiling water
2	tsp. packed brown sugar
1	Earl Grey tea bag
2	Tbsp. (1 oz.) dark rum
1½	tsp. Spiced Butter

1. In a mug stir together boiling water and brown sugar until sugar is dissolved. Add tea bag; steep 5 minutes. Remove and discard tea bag. Add rum. Top with Spiced Butter. Makes 1 serving.
PER SERVING *139 cal., 6 g fat (4 g sat. fat), 15 mg chol., 51 mg sodium, 6 g carb., 0 g fiber, 6 g sugars, 0 g pro.*
Spiced Butter In a small bowl combine ½ cup softened butter and 1 teaspoon pumpkin pie spice. Roll into a log and wrap in plastic wrap. Chill until firm.

WHITE CHOCOLATE MUDSLIDES

START TO FINISH 15 minutes

1	cup white chocolate baking pieces
2	Tbsp. milk
3½	cups vanilla ice cream
¼	cup coffee-flavor liqueur
¼	cup Irish cream liqueur
	Fresh raspberries

1. Place white chocolate pieces in a small microwave-safe bowl. Microwave on high 30 to 60 seconds or until melted, stirring twice. Add milk and stir until smooth. Cool slightly.
2. Place ice cream, liqueurs, and white chocolate mixture in a blender. Cover and blend until smooth. Pour into martini glasses; garnish with raspberries on skewers. Makes 5 servings.
PER SERVING *692 cal., 37 g fat (27 g sat. fat), 138 mg chol., 145 mg sodium, 74 g carb., 0 g fiber, 65 g sugars, 6 g pro.*

CHEESY ROSEMARY AND PECAN SNACK MIX

PREP 5 minutes
BAKE 30 minutes at 300°F

3	cups pecan halves
2	cups oyster crackers
2	cups square white cheddar cheese crackers
1½	cups freshly grated Parmesan cheese
1	cup pumpkin seeds
2	Tbsp. packed brown sugar
2	Tbsp. chopped fresh rosemary
2	tsp. crushed red pepper
4	cloves garlic, minced
½	cup melted butter

1. Preheat oven to 300°F. In a large bowl combine pecan halves, oyster crackers, cheddar cheese crackers, Parmesan, pumpkin seeds, brown sugar, rosemary, crushed red pepper, and garlic. Drizzle in melted butter; stir gently to coat. Spread on a 15×10-inch baking sheet.
2. Bake 15 minutes; stir. Bake 15 minutes more. Cool completely. Store in an airtight container. Makes 21 servings.
PER SERVING *262 cal., 22 g fat (6 g sat. fat), 17 mg chol., 235 mg sodium, 13 g carb., 2 g fiber, 2 g sugars, 6 g pro.*

GINGER-ORANGE PUNCH

START TO FINISH 10 minutes

1	pint orange sherbet
½	cup grenadine
½	cup orange juice
6	cups chilled ginger ale
	Ice cubes

WHITE CHOCOLATE
MUDSLIDES

EARL GREY HOT
BUTTERED RUM

GINGER-ORANGE
PUNCH

Sweet & Savory Brunch

Build a brunch with these recipes for cinnamon rolls and twists, pancakes and waffles, hearty egg burritos and bakes, and warming latte and cocoa.

SWEET POTATO
PANCAKES, PAGE 49

CINNAMON ROLL
TWISTS, PAGE 44

GINGERBREAD CINNAMON ROLLS

PREP 30 minutes
RISE 1 hour 15 minutes
STAND 10 minutes
BAKE 25 minutes at 375°F
COOL 10 minutes

3¾ to 4¼ cups all-purpose flour
4   tsp. ground ginger
4   tsp. ground cinnamon
½   tsp. ground cloves
1   pkg. active dry yeast
¾   cup milk
1   cup mashed potato*
⅓   cup butter
⅓   cup molasses
1   tsp. salt
2   eggs
½   cup packed brown sugar
¼   cup butter, softened
1   recipe Spiced Browned Butter Frosting

1. In a large bowl stir together 1½ cups flour, 3 teaspoons ginger, 1 teaspoon cinnamon, ¼ teaspoon cloves, and the yeast. In a 2-quart saucepan heat and stir milk, mashed potato, ⅓ cup butter, the molasses, and salt just until warm (120°F to 130°F) and butter is almost melted. Add milk mixture and eggs to flour mixture. Mix until smooth. Add about 2 cups flour and stir in as much as you can.

2. Turn dough out onto a lightly floured surface. Knead in enough remaining flour to make a moderately soft dough that is smooth and elastic (3 to 5 minutes total). Shape dough into a ball. Place in a lightly greased bowl, turning to grease surface of dough. Cover; let rise until double in size (45 to 60 minutes).

3. Punch dough down. Turn out onto a lightly floured surface. Cover; let rest 10 minutes. Lightly grease a 13×9-inch baking pan.

4. For filling, in a small bowl stir together brown sugar and the remaining ginger, cinnamon, and cloves.

5. Roll dough into an 18×12-inch rectangle. Spread with softened butter and sprinkle with filling, leaving 1 inch unfilled along one long side. Roll up tightly, starting from filled long side and pinching seam to seal. Cut into 12 slices; arrange in pan, cut sides up. Cover; let rise until nearly double in size (30 minutes).

6. Preheat oven to 375°F. Bake 25 to 30 minutes or until golden. Cool in pan on a wire rack 10 minutes; invert to remove from pan. Invert again. Spread with Spiced Browned Butter Frosting. Makes 12 servings.

Spiced Browned Butter Frosting
In a 1- to 1½-quart saucepan melt ¾ cup butter over low until butter turns a delicate light brown, stirring occasionally. Let cool slightly. In a large bowl combine 3⅔ cups powdered sugar, 1 teaspoon ground ginger, ½ teaspoon ground cinnamon, dash ground cloves, 2 tablespoons milk, and 1 teaspoon vanilla. Stir in the brown butter until combined. Add additional milk, 1 teaspoon a time, to reach spreading consistency. Makes 1¾ cups.

***Tip** Prick a 10-oz. potato all over with a fork. Microwave on high 5 to 7 minutes or until tender. Halve potato and scoop pulp out of skin into a small bowl; discard skin. Mash potato pulp with a potato masher or a mixer on low. Measure 1 cup mashed potato. Or prepare instant mashed potato flakes according to package directions to make 1 cup. Or used leftover mashed potatoes.

Star-Shape Gingerbread Cinnamon Rolls Prepare dough as directed. Line 2 baking sheets with parchment paper. After punching dough down, divide into

8 equal portions. Let rest 10 minutes. For each star, on a lightly floured surface roll one portion of dough to a 10-inch round. Place on prepared sheet. Brush with melted butter. Sprinkle with a slightly rounded tablespoon of filling mixture. Repeat twice, stacking rounds. Top with a fourth dough round. Brush with melted butter. Use a 2½-inch round cutter to slightly indent the center of dough stack. Leaving cutter at center, use a sharp knife to cut 16 strips, from cutter to edge of stack. Twist 2 adjacent strips twice, twisting each in opposite direction. Pinch twists together at the ends to form star tip. Repeat to make 8 star tips. Remove cutter. Repeat with remaining dough and filling. Let rise, brush with additional melted butter, and bake at 375°F 20 minutes or until golden. Omit frosting. If desired, dust with powdered sugar. Makes 2 stars.
PER SERVING *567 cal., 22 g fat (14 g sat. fat), 87 mg chol., 385 mg sodium, 87 g carb., 2 g fiber, 53 g sugars, 7 g pro.*

BACON-CARAMEL ROLLS

PREP 40 minutes
BAKE 15 minutes at 400°F plus 25 minutes at 375°F
RISE 1 hour
COOL 5 minutes

8	slices bacon
½	cup butter, melted
¾	cup packed brown sugar
¼	cup light-color corn syrup
¾	cup chopped pecans
⅔	cup packed brown sugar
1	Tbsp. ground cinnamon
2	16-oz. loaves frozen white bread dough or sweet roll dough, thawed
6	Tbsp. butter, softened
¾	cup raisins (optional)

1. Preheat oven to 400°F. Line a 15×10-inch baking pan with foil. Lay bacon in pan in a single layer. Bake about 15 minutes or until crisp; drain on paper towels. Coarsely chop bacon.
2. Grease a 13×9-inch baking pan. In a medium bowl stir together melted butter, ¾ cup packed brown sugar, and the corn syrup. Stir in chopped pecans and half the chopped bacon. Spread mixture in prepared pan.

3. Stir together ⅔ cup brown sugar and the cinnamon. On a lightly floured surface, roll each loaf of dough into a 12×8-inch rectangle, stopping to let dough relax while rolling, if needed. Spread softened butter on dough rectangles. Sprinkle with brown sugar-cinnamon mixture, the remaining bacon, and, if desired, raisins.
4. From a long side, roll each rectangle into a spiral. Pinch dough to seal seams. Slice each roll into eight pieces. Arrange pieces, cut sides up, in prepared pan.

Cover; let rise in a warm place until nearly double in size (about 1 hour).
5. Preheat oven to 375°F. Bake 25 to 30 minutes or until rolls are golden brown and sound hollow when gently tapped. If needed, cover rolls loosely with foil the last 10 minutes of baking to prevent overbrowning. Cool rolls in pan 5 minutes. Invert rolls onto a platter. Serve warm. Makes 16 servings.
PER SERVING *378 cal., 17 g fat (7 g sat. fat), 31 mg chol., 411 mg sodium, 51 g carb., 1 g fiber, 26 g sugars, 5 g pro.*

BACON-CARAMEL ROLLS

CINNAMON ROLL TWISTS

PREP 45 minutes
RISE 1 hour 15 minutes
STAND 10 minutes
BAKE 25 minutes at 375°F
COOL 10 minutes

4¼ to 4¾ cups all-purpose flour
1 pkg. active dry yeast
1 cup milk
1 cup mashed cooked potato (tip, page 42)
⅓ cup butter
⅓ cup granulated sugar
1 tsp. salt
2 eggs
½ cup packed brown sugar
⅓ cup snipped dried tart cherries, golden raisins, dried apricots, or dried cranberries
⅓ cup chopped toasted pecans (tip, page 24)
1 Tbsp. ground cinnamon
¼ cup butter, softened
   Nonstick cooking spray
1 recipe Cream Cheese Icing

1. In a large bowl combine 1½ cups of the flour and the yeast; set aside. In a medium saucepan heat and stir milk, potato, ⅓ cup butter, the granulated sugar, and salt just until warm (120°F to 130°F) and butter is almost melted. Add to flour mixture; add eggs. Beat with a mixer on low to medium 30 seconds, scraping sides of bowl constantly. Beat on high 3 minutes. Stir in as much remaining flour as you can.

2. Turn dough out onto a lightly floured surface. Knead in enough of the remaining flour to make a moderately soft dough that is smooth and elastic (3 to 5 minutes total). Shape dough into a ball. Place in a lightly greased bowl; turn once to grease surface of dough. Cover; let rise in a warm place until double in size (45 to 60 minutes).

3. Punch dough down. Turn out onto a lightly floured surface. Cover and let rest 10 minutes. Meanwhile, lightly grease two 9-inch round foil pans; set aside. For filling, in a small bowl stir together brown sugar, cherries, pecans, and cinnamon.

4. Divide dough in half. Roll one half into a 20×9-inch rectangle. Spread 2 tablespoons of the softened butter over dough and sprinkle with half the filling. Roll up rectangle, starting from a long side. Pinch dough to seal seams. Slice the roll in half lengthwise. Place halves side-by-side, cut sides up. Twist halves together. Shape into a ring; pinch and seal ends together. Place ring in one prepared pan. Coat the outside of a 6-ounce custard cup with nonstick spray. Place the cup, right side up, in the center of the ring. Repeat with remaining dough, butter, and filling. Cover and let rise in a warm place until nearly double in size (about 30 minutes).

5. Preheat oven to 375°F. Bake 25 to 30 minutes or until golden. Cool 10 minutes in pan on a wire rack. Remove custard cups from centers of rings. Spread with Cream Cheese Icing. Serve warm. Makes 12 servings.

Make Ahead Prepare as directed through Step 4, except do not let rise after shaping. Cover loosely with oiled waxed paper, then with plastic wrap. Chill 2 to 24 hours. Before baking, let chilled twists stand, covered, 30 minutes at room temperature. Uncover and bake as directed.

CINNAMON ROLL TWISTS

Cream Cheese Icing In a medium mixing bowl beat one 3-ounce package softened cream cheese, 2 tablespoons softened butter, and 1 teaspoon vanilla with a mixer on medium until smooth. Gradually add 2½ cups powdered sugar, beating well. Beat in enough milk, 1 teaspoon at a time, to reach desired consistency.

PER SERVING *513 cal., 17 g fat (9 g sat. fat), 69 mg chol., 341 mg sodium, 83 g carb., 3 g fiber, 44 g sugars, 8 g pro.*

CHOCOLATE-PEANUT BUTTER BAKED DONUTS

PREP 25 minutes
CHILL 2 hours
BAKE 12 minutes at 350°F
COOL 5 minutes

Nonstick cooking spray
1¼ cups all-purpose flour
⅔ cup packed brown sugar
¼ cup unsweetened cocoa powder
¾ tsp. baking soda
¼ tsp. salt
⅓ cup cold butter
⅔ cup milk
1 egg, lightly beaten
1 tsp. vanilla
¼ cup chopped dark (60% cacao) chocolate (2 oz.)
½ oz. chopped semisweet chocolate (2 Tbsp.)
1½ Tbsp. canola oil
1 Tbsp. butter
1 Tbsp. peanut butter
Chopped peanuts

1. Coat 12 indentations of a standard-size donut pan or 24 indentations of a mini-size donut pan with cooking spray. In a medium bowl combine flour, brown sugar, cocoa powder, baking soda, and salt. Use a pastry blender to cut in ⅓ cup butter until mixture resembles fine crumbs.

2. In a small bowl combine milk, egg, and vanilla. Add egg mixture to flour mixture, stirring just until combined (do not overmix).

3. Spoon batter into a pastry bag fitted with a ½-inch round tip. Pipe batter into prepared pans. Lightly coat a sheet of plastic wrap with cooking spray. Place over filled pan, coated side down. Chill 2 to 24 hours.

CHOCOLATE-PEANUT BUTTER BAKED DONUTS

4. Preheat oven to 350°F. Remove wrap; bake standard-size donuts 12 to 15 minutes or until donuts spring back when lightly touched. (Bake mini donuts 8 to 10 minutes.) Cool in pan on a wire rack 5 minutes. Carefully invert pan onto a wire rack.

5. For glaze, in a small saucepan combine chopped chocolates, oil, 1 tablespoon butter, and the peanut butter. Cook and stir over medium until glaze is smooth.

6. Dip each donut top into glaze. Return to wire rack and sprinkle with chopped peanuts. Let stand until glaze is set. Makes 12 servings.

PER SERVING *236 cal., 13 g fat (6 g sat. fat), 33 mg chol., 210 mg sodium, 28 g carb., 2 g fiber, 15 g sugars, 4 g pro.*

CHERRY-CHOCOLATE SCONES

PREP 20 minutes
BAKE 12 minutes at 400°F

2½ cups all-purpose flour
2 Tbsp. sugar
1 Tbsp. baking powder
¼ tsp. salt
⅓ cup butter
2 eggs, lightly beaten
¾ cup whipping cream
¼ cup snipped dried cherries
¼ cup miniature semisweet chocolate pieces
½ tsp. orange zest (optional)
1 recipe Orange Drizzle

1. Preheat oven to 400°F. In a large bowl stir together flour, sugar, baking powder, and salt. Using a pastry blender, cut in butter until mixture resembles coarse crumbs. Make a well in the center of flour mixture; set aside.
2. In a medium bowl combine eggs, whipping cream, dried cherries, chocolate pieces, and, if desired, orange zest. Add egg mixture all at once to flour mixture. Using a fork, stir just until moistened.
3. Turn dough out onto a lightly floured surface. Knead dough by folding and gently pressing 10 to 12 strokes or until dough is nearly smooth. Divide dough in half. Pat or lightly roll each dough half into a 6-inch circle. Cut each circle into six wedges.
4. Place dough wedges 2 inches apart on an ungreased baking sheet. Brush wedges with additional whipping cream.
5. Bake 12 to 14 minutes or until golden. Cool slightly on baking sheet. Drizzle with Orange Drizzle. Serve warm or at room temperature. Makes 12 servings.

Orange Drizzle In a small bowl stir together 1 cup powdered sugar, 1 tablespoon orange juice, and ¼ teaspoon vanilla. If necessary, stir in additional orange juice, 1 teaspoon at a time, to reach drizzling consistency.
PER SERVING 291 cal., 14 g fat (8 g sat. fat), 67 mg chol., 203 mg sodium, 38 g carb., 1 g fiber, 16 g sugars, 4 g pro.

CARAMEL APPLE BAKED FRENCH TOAST

PREP 25 minutes
BAKE 35 minutes at 350°F
STAND 10 minutes

Nonstick cooking spray
2 9-oz. loaves baguette-style French bread
1 large red-skin cooking apple, such as Jonathan or Gala, cored and chopped
1 Tbsp. lemon juice
4 eggs, lightly beaten
1 cup milk
½ cup caramel-flavor ice cream topping
1 tsp. vanilla
½ tsp. ground cinnamon
¼ tsp. ground ginger
⅛ tsp. ground nutmeg

1. Preheat oven to 350°F. Coat a 2-quart rectangular baking dish with cooking spray. Trim ends off baguettes. Cut remaining baguettes crosswise into ½-inch slices. Arrange bread slices, standing on edge, in prepared dish. Top bread with apple. Brush apple with lemon juice.
2. In a medium bowl whisk together eggs, milk, 2 tablespoons ice cream topping, the vanilla, cinnamon, ginger, and nutmeg. Slowly pour egg mixture over bread, pouring between each slice.
3. Bake, uncovered, 35 to 40 minutes or until heated through, top is golden brown, and apple is tender. Let stand 10 minutes before serving. Drizzle with remaining ice cream topping. Makes 12 servings.
PER SERVING 202 cal., 3 g fat (1 g sat. fat), 64 mg chol., 326 mg sodium, 36 g carb., 1 g fiber, 13 g sugars, 7 g pro.

CHERRY-CHOCOLATE SCONES

GINGERBREAD WAFFLES WITH HOT LEMON CURD SAUCE

PREP 45 minutes
COOK per waffle-maker directions

- ½ cup sugar
- 1 tsp. all-purpose flour
- ½ cup water
- 2 egg yolks, lightly beaten
- 2 Tbsp. butter, cut up
- 1 tsp. lemon zest
- 3 Tbsp. lemon juice
- 2 cups all-purpose flour
- 1 tsp. ground cinnamon
- 1½ tsp. baking soda
- 1½ tsp. ground ginger
- ½ tsp. ground cloves
- ½ tsp. salt
- 3 egg yolks, lightly beaten
- 1 cup molasses
- ½ cup buttermilk
- ½ cup butter, melted
- 2 egg whites

1. For Hot Lemon Curd Sauce, in a medium saucepan stir together sugar and 1 teaspoon flour. Stir in the water. Cook and stir over medium until thickened and bubbly. Remove from heat.

2. Stir half the sugar-flour mixture into the 2 egg yolks, stirring constantly. Return egg mixture to saucepan. Cook, stirring constantly, over medium until sauce comes to a gentle boil. Cook and stir 2 minutes more. Remove from heat. Add butter pieces, stirring until melted. Stir in lemon zest and juice. Use immediately or cover surface with plastic wrap until ready to serve.

3. For waffles, in a large bowl combine 2 cups flour, the cinnamon, baking soda, ginger, cloves, and salt; make a well in center. In a bowl combine the 3 egg yolks, molasses, buttermilk, and melted butter. Add egg mixture all at once to flour mixture. Stir until moistened.

4. In a small bowl beat egg whites with a mixer on medium 1 to 1½ minutes or until stiff peaks form (tips stand straight). Gently fold beaten egg whites into batter, leaving a few fluffs of egg white.

5. Bake waffles in a preheated, lightly greased waffle baker according to manufacturer directions. Serve with Hot Lemon Curd Sauce. Makes 12 servings.

PER SERVING *152 cal., 6 g fat (3 g sat. fat), 51 mg chol., 186 mg sodium, 23 g carb., 0 g fiber, 12 g sugars, 2 g pro.*

CARAMEL APPLE BAKED FRENCH TOAST

GINGERBREAD WAFFLES WITH HOT LEMON CURD SAUCE

MAPLE-TANGERINE CREPES

DUTCH BABY WITH CARAMELIZED APPLES

MAPLE-TANGERINE CREPES

START TO FINISH 25 minutes

⅓ cup pure maple syrup
1 Tbsp. cornstarch
1 tsp. tangerine zest or orange zest
1 cup tangerine juice or orange juice
1 egg
¾ cup fat-free milk
½ cup all-purpose flour
1 Tbsp. canola oil
2 tsp. sugar
½ cup mascarpone cheese, softened
2 Tbsp. pure maple syrup
Tangerine or orange slices (optional)

1. For sauce, in a small saucepan combine the ⅓ cup maple syrup and the cornstarch. Stir in tangerine juice. Cook and stir over medium until thickened and bubbly. Cook and stir 2 minutes more. Set aside.

2. In a medium bowl combine egg, milk, flour, oil, sugar, and tangerine zest; whisk until smooth.

3. Heat a lightly greased 8-inch skillet over medium-high; remove from heat. Spoon in 2 tablespoons batter; lift and tilt skillet to spread batter evenly. Return to heat; cook 1 to 2 minutes or until browned on one side only. Invert skillet over paper towels; remove crepe. Repeat with remaining batter, greasing skillet occasionally. If crepes brown too quickly, reduce heat to medium.

4. For filling, in a small bowl combine mascarpone cheese and the 2 tablespoons maple syrup. Spread unbrowned side of each crepe with 1 tablespoon filling; fold crepe into quarters. Serve crepes with sauce. If desired, garnish with tangerine slices. Makes 10 servings.

Make Ahead Prepare crepes; cool completely. Layer crepes between sheets of waxed paper or parchment paper, wrap in plastic wrap, and place in a resealable plastic bag; seal. Refrigerate up to 3 days or freeze up to 3 months. To use, thaw at room temperature if frozen.

PER SERVING *149 cal., 7 g fat (3 g sat. fat), 35 mg chol., 21 mg sodium, 19 g carb., 1 g fiber, 14 g sugars, 2 g pro.*

DUTCH BABY WITH CARAMELIZED APPLES

PREP 20 minutes
BAKE 15 minutes at 425°F

3   eggs, lightly beaten
½   cup milk
½   cup all-purpose flour
1   Tbsp. granulated sugar
½   tsp. vanilla
¼   tsp. salt
¼   tsp. ground cinnamon
3   Tbsp. butter
1⅓ cups thinly sliced apple
2   Tbsp. brown sugar
2   Tbsp. maple syrup
    Powdered sugar

1. Preheat oven to 425°F. For batter, in a medium bowl combine eggs and milk. Whisk in flour, granulated sugar, vanilla, salt, and cinnamon.
2. In a 9- or 10-inch oven-going skillet melt 1½ tablespoons butter over medium. Pour batter into skillet. Bake 15 minutes or until light brown and puffed.

3. Meanwhile, in a medium saucepan melt remaining 1½ tablespoons butter over medium-high. Add apples; cook, stirring, 5 minutes or until crisp-tender and browning on edges. Stir in brown sugar and syrup; cook 2 to 3 minutes or until tender. Serve Dutch baby with apples and, if desired, dust with powdered sugar. Makes 4 servings.
PER SERVING *287 cal., 13 g fat (7 g sat. fat), 165 mg chol., 285 mg sodium, 35 g carb., 1 g fiber, 21 g sugars, 8 g pro.*

SWEET POTATO PANCAKES

PREP 10 minutes
COOK 2 to 4 minutes per pancake

1¼ cups all-purpose flour
½   cup cornmeal
2   Tbsp. packed brown sugar
1   Tbsp. baking powder
1   tsp. salt
1   tsp. ground cinnamon
¼   tsp. ground nutmeg

2   eggs, lightly beaten
1¾ cups milk
½   cup mashed sweet potato
2   Tbsp. vegetable oil
    Coarsely chopped pecans and/or maple syrup (optional)

1. In a bowl stir together flour, cornmeal, brown sugar, baking powder, salt, cinnamon, and nutmeg. In a bowl combine eggs, milk, sweet potato, and oil. Add egg mixture all at once to flour mixture. Stir just until moistened.
2. For each pancake, pour about ¼ cup batter onto a hot, lightly greased griddle or heavy skillet, spreading batter if necessary. Cook over medium 1 to 2 minutes on each side or until pancakes are golden brown. Flip when surfaces are bubbly and edges are slightly dry. Serve warm. If desired, top with pecans and serve with syrup. Makes 8 servings.
PER SERVING *208 cal., 6 fat (2 g sat. fat), 51 mg chol., 477 mg sodium, 32 g carb., 2 g fiber, 7 g sugars, 6 g pro.*

SWEET POTATO PANCAKES

LEMON RICOTTA PANCAKES WITH WARM BLUEBERRY COMPOTE

LEMON RICOTTA PANCAKES WITH WARM BLUEBERRY COMPOTE

PREP 20 minutes
COOK 20 minutes

½ cup granulated sugar
1 tsp. cornstarch
2 cups fresh or frozen blueberries
¼ cup water
1 10-oz. jar lemon curd
1½ tsp. orange juice
Salt
1½ tsp. butter
¼ tsp. vanilla
2 cups all-purpose flour
2 Tbsp. granulated sugar
2 tsp. baking powder
½ tsp. salt
1 tsp. lemon zest
2 eggs, separated
1 cup whole milk ricotta cheese

1½ cups whole milk
Powdered sugar

1. For blueberry compote, in a medium saucepan combine ½ cup granulated sugar and the cornstarch. Add blueberries, the water, 2 tablespoons of the lemon curd, the orange juice, and a pinch of salt. Bring mixture to boiling, stirring constantly. Reduce heat; simmer, uncovered, over medium to medium-low until blueberries are tender but not broken down and mixture is slightly thickened, stirring occasionally. Remove saucepan from heat; stir in butter and vanilla. Set aside to cool slightly.
2. For pancakes, in a medium bowl combine flour, 2 tablespoons granulated sugar, the baking powder, ½ teaspoon salt, and the lemon zest. In a large bowl combine egg yolks and ricotta cheese. Fold in flour mixture alternately with milk. Set aside.

3. In a small bowl beat the egg whites on medium-high with a mixer until stiff peaks form (tips stand straight). Gently fold egg whites into batter.
4. Pour about ¼ cup batter onto a hot, lightly greased griddle or heavy skillet. Spread batter, if necessary. Cook over medium 2 minutes on each side or until pancakes are golden brown. Flip when surfaces are bubbly and edges are slightly dry.
5. To serve, place three warm pancakes on each plate. Spread about 1 tablespoon of the remaining lemon curd on each pancake. Sprinkle with powdered sugar and spoon some blueberry compote over pancakes. Makes 5 servings
PER SERVING *672 cal., 15 g fat (8 g sat. fat), 152 mg chol., 560 mg sodium, 121 g carb., 8 g fiber, 73 g sugars, 16 g pro.*

SLOW-TOASTED GRANOLA

PREP 20 minutes
SLOW COOK 2 hours 30 minutes (high)

Nonstick cooking spray
5   cups regular rolled oats
½   cup sunflower kernels
2   Tbsp. ground flaxseeds or wheat germ
½   cup honey
½   cup applesauce
¼   cup canola oil
¼   cup peanut butter
1   tsp. ground cinnamon
½   cup golden raisins
¼   cup chopped pitted whole dates

1. Lightly coat a 3½- or 4-quart slow cooker with cooking spray. Combine oats, sunflower kernels, and flaxseeds in cooker. In a small bowl whisk together honey, applesauce, oil, peanut butter, and cinnamon. Add honey mixture to cooker; stir to mix.
2. Off-set the lid on cooker to vent. Cook on high 2½ hours or until oat mixture is toasted, stirring every 30 minutes. Spread oat mixture on aluminum foil or parchment paper to cool. Sprinkle with raisins and dates; toss gently to combine. Makes 16 servings.
PER SERVING *234 cal., 10 g fat (1 g sat. fat), 0 mg chol., 35 mg sodium, 35 g carb., 4 g fiber, 15 g sugars, 5 g pro.*

PEANUT BUTTER, BANANA, AND BACON OATMEAL

PREP 15 minutes
COOK 25 minutes
BAKE 10 minutes at 400°F

4   cups milk
1   cup steel-cut oats
¼   tsp. salt
½   cup crunchy peanut butter
2   Tbsp. packed brown sugar
2   bananas, peeled and cut into chunks
4   slices bacon, crisp-cooked and crumbled
2   Tbsp. flaxseeds
2   Tbsp. grape jelly, melted
½   cup chopped strawberries

1. In a large saucepan bring milk just to boiling over medium (watch carefully so milk doesn't boil). Add oats and salt.

Reduce heat to medium-low; simmer, uncovered, 25 to 30 minutes or until oats are tender and mixture is thickened and creamy, stirring frequently to prevent sticking. Remove from heat.
2. Preheat oven to 400°F. Stir peanut butter, brown sugar, bananas, bacon, and flaxseeds into oats. Spoon into a 9-inch cast-iron skillet or 1½-quart casserole. Bake 10 to 15 minutes or until heated through. Stir in jelly. Top with strawberries and additional bacon. Drizzle with additional jelly. Makes 6 servings.
PER SERVING *418 cal., 19 g fat (5 g sat. fat), 18 mg chol., 371 mg sodium, 51 g carb., 7 g fiber, 23 g sugars, 17 g pro.*

SLOW-TOASTED GRANOLA

PEANUT BUTTER, BANANA, AND BACON OATMEAL

BACON AND EGG BURRITOS

START TO FINISH 45 minutes

- 3 Tbsp. butter
- 3 cups refrigerated shredded hash brown potatoes
- 2 cloves garlic, minced
- ¼ tsp. ground cumin
- 8 slices bacon, crisp-cooked, drained, and crumbled
- 6 eggs, lightly beaten
- ⅓ cup milk
- ¼ tsp. salt
- ⅛ tsp. black pepper
- 8 10-inch flour tortillas
- 1 4-oz. can diced green chile peppers, drained
- ½ cup red and/or green salsa
- 1¼ cups shredded Colby and Monterey Jack cheese (5 oz.)

1. In a large nonstick skillet heat 2 tablespoons of the butter over medium until melted. Stir in potatoes, garlic, and cumin. Spread in an even layer; press down lightly with a spatula. Cool 6 to 7 minutes or until golden on bottom. Turn potatoes over; spread evenly and press down lightly. Cook 6 to 8 minutes more or until golden and crisp on bottom. Stir in bacon. Remove from skillet; keep warm.

2. In a medium bowl combine eggs, milk, salt, and black pepper. In the same skillet heat remaining 1 tablespoon butter over medium until melted. Pour in egg mixture. Cook, without stirring, until mixture begins to set on bottom and around edges. Using a spatula or large spoon, lift and fold the partially cooked egg mixture so uncooked portion flows underneath. Continue cooking 2 to 3 minutes or until egg is cooked through but still glossy and moist. Immediately remove from heat.

3. Stack tortillas and wrap in microwave-safe paper towels. Microwave on high 1 minute or until heated through. Divide potato mixture among tortillas, just below center of each tortilla. Divide cooked eggs, green chile peppers, and salsa among tortillas; sprinkle with cheese. Fold bottom edge of each tortilla up and over filling, fold in sides, and roll from bottom. Makes 8 servings.

PER SERVING *492 cal., 23 g fat (11 g sat. fat), 180 mg chol., 1,050 mg sodium, 51 g carb., 4 g fiber, 3 g sugars, 20 g pro.*

BACON AND EGG BURRITOS

EGG AND SAUSAGE BREAD BAKES

PREP 30 minutes
BAKE 35 minutes at 350°F
STAND 5 minutes

2   14×4-inch unsliced loaves Italian or French bread
8   oz. uncooked sweet or mild Italian sausage, casings removed if present
¾   cup chopped red or yellow sweet pepper
½   cup sliced green onions
10 eggs, lightly beaten
⅔   cup heavy cream or half-and-half
¼   cup chopped fresh basil
½   tsp. salt
1½ cups shredded Fontina, mozzarella, or provolone cheese (6 oz.)

1. Preheat oven to 350°F. Line a large baking sheet with parchment paper. Using a serrated knife, cut a wedge into tops of loaves. Using a spoon, remove insides. Arrange bread shells on prepared baking sheet.
2. In a 10-inch skillet cook sausage and sweet pepper over medium 8 minutes or until sausage is browned and pepper is just tender, stirring in green onions during the last 1 minute of cooking. Drain off fat.
3. In a large bowl combine eggs, cream, basil, and salt. Stir in sausage mixture and 1 cup of the cheese.
4. Pour egg mixture into bread shells. Sprinkle with remaining ½ cup cheese. Bake 35 to 40 minutes or until eggs are set (160°F). Let stand 5 minutes before slicing. If desired, sprinkle with additional basil. Makes 10 servings.
PER SERVING 490 cal., 23 g fat (11 g sat. fat), 245 mg chol., 977 mg sodium, 45 g carb., 0 g fiber, 1 g sugars, 20 g pro.

EGG AND SAUSAGE BREAD BAKES

MONTE CRISTO
BREAKFAST
CASSEROLE

MONTE CRISTO BREAKFAST CASSEROLE

PREP 30 minutes
CHILL 8 hours
BAKE 35 minutes at 350°F
STAND 10 minutes

2½ cups milk
8 eggs
3 cloves garlic, minced
½ tsp. salt
¼ tsp. black pepper
1 1- to 1½-lb. round loaf country Italian bread, cut into ten ½-inch-thick slices
¼ cup Dijon mustard
8 oz. thinly sliced cooked ham
1½ cups shredded Gruyère or Swiss cheese (6 oz.)
¼ cup butter, softened
 Powdered sugar

1. Grease a 3-quart baking dish. In a large bowl whisk together milk, eggs, garlic, salt, and pepper.
2. Spread half the bread slices with mustard; top with ham and half the cheese. Spread remaining bread slices with butter; place buttered sides down on cheese. Cut each sandwich diagonally into four triangles. Arrange points up in prepared baking dish. Pour egg mixture over sandwiches. Sprinkle with remaining cheese. Cover and chill 8 hours or overnight.
3. Preheat oven to 350°F. Uncover dish. Bake 35 minutes or until golden and egg mixture is set. Let stand 10 minutes before serving. Sprinkle with powdered sugar. Makes 12 servings.
PER SERVING *319 cal., 17 g fat (9 g sat. fat), 170 mg chol., 804 mg sodium, 23 g carb., 1 g fiber, 5 g sugars, 17 g pro.*

CHEESE SOUFFLÉ

PREP 50 minutes
BAKE 40 minutes at 350°F

¼ cup butter
¼ cup all-purpose flour
¼ tsp. dry mustard
 Dash cayenne pepper
1 cup milk
2 cups shredded cheddar, Colby, Havarti, and/or process Swiss cheese (8 oz.)
4 egg yolks, room temperature
4 egg whites, room temperature

1. Preheat oven to 350°F. For cheese sauce, in a medium saucepan melt butter over medium. Stir in flour, dry mustard, and cayenne pepper. Add milk all at once. Cook and stir until thickened and bubbly. Remove from heat. A little at a time, add cheese, stirring until cheese is melted. In a medium bowl beat egg yolks with a fork. Slowly add cheese sauce to egg yolks, stirring constantly. Cool slightly.
2. In a large bowl beat egg whites with a mixer on medium to high until stiff peaks form (tips stand straight). Gently fold about 1 cup of the beaten egg whites into cheese sauce. Gradually pour cheese sauce over remaining beaten egg whites, folding to combine. Pour into an ungreased 1½-quart ceramic loaf pan or 2-quart soufflé dish.
3. Bake 40 minutes or until a knife inserted near center comes out clean. Serve immediately. Makes 4 servings.
PER SERVING *459 cal., 36 g fat (22 g sat. fat), 305 mg chol., 521 mg sodium, 10 g carb., 0 g fiber, 4 g sugars, 23 g pro.*

CHEESE SOUFFLÉ

FRICO FRIED EGG AND CHEESE BREAKFAST SANDWICHES

POTATO, LEEK, AND SAUSAGE BREAD PUDDING

PREP 10 minutes
BAKE 50 minutes at 350°F
COOK 35 minutes

4   Tbsp. unsalted butter, melted
1   15-oz. pkg. stale potato bread
     rolls, cut into 1½-inch cubes
2   Tbsp. olive oil
4   large leeks (2½ to 3 lb.), dark
     greens trimmed, white and light
     green parts thinly sliced
1   tsp. kosher salt
½   tsp. black pepper
12   oz. sweet or spicy Italian sausage,
     casings removed
6   large eggs
2   cups whole milk
½   cup heavy cream

1. Preheat oven to 350°F. Brush a
3-quart baking dish with 1 tablespoon
melted butter. Divide bread cubes
between two large baking sheets.
Drizzle with remaining 3 tablespoons
melted butter and toss to coat. Toast
until lightly golden, 10 to 12 minutes.
2. Heat oil in a large skillet over
medium-low. Add leeks, ½ teaspoon
salt, and ¼ teaspoon black pepper.
Cook, stirring occasionally, until leeks
are very tender, about 25 minutes.
Transfer leeks to a plate.
3. Add sausage to skillet and cook over
medium-high, breaking up sausage with
a spoon, until browned and cooked
through, 10 to 12 minutes. Let cool a
few minutes.
4. In an extra-large bowl whisk eggs,
milk, cream, the remaining ½ teaspoon
salt and ¼ teaspoon pepper. Add
cooled bread cubes, leeks, and
sausage; toss gently. Set aside 5 minutes
to allow the bread to absorb most of
the liquid. Toss mixture again; spread in
prepared dish. Cover and refrigerate
until ready to bake. Bake, uncovered, at
350°F until slightly puffed and golden,
about 40 minutes. Serve warm. Makes
10 servings.

PER SERVING *364 cal., 20 g fat
(9 g sat. fat), 152 mg chol., 540 mg sodium,
29 g carb., 3 g fiber, 8 g sugars, 17 g pro.*

FRICO FRIED EGG AND CHEESE BREAKFAST SANDWICHES

START TO FINISH 20 minutes

½   cup shredded Parmesan or Grana
     Padano cheese (2 oz.)
4   eggs
     Salt and black pepper
4   slices provolone cheese
4   English muffins, split and toasted
     Pesto, aïoli, or Dijon mustard
¼   cup thinly sliced oil-packed dried
     tomatoes
1   cup baby arugula

1. Heat an extra-large griddle or
nonstick skillet over low. For each
frico, sprinkle 2 tablespoons Parmesan
cheese into a 4-inch circle on hot
griddle. Cook 1 minute or just until
cheese begins to melt.
2. Break eggs onto cheese rounds;
sprinkle with salt and pepper. Cook
4 to 5 minutes or until egg whites are
completely set and yolks are desired
doneness. Top with provolone cheese;
cook 3 minutes or until cheese is melted.
3. Spread English muffin bottoms
with pesto, if desired; top with dried
tomatoes. Add eggs, arugula, and
muffin tops. Makes 4 servings.

PER SERVING *380 cal., 18 g fat (7 g sat.
fat), 207 mg chol., 760 mg sodium,
35 g carb., 1 g fiber, 3 g sugars, 19 g pro.*

POTATO, LEEK AND
SAUSAGE BREAD PUDDING

HASH-BROWN-CRUSTED QUICHE

PREP 35 minutes
COOK 20 minutes
BAKE 50 minutes at 325°F
STAND 10 minutes

1¾ lb. russet potatoes
½ tsp. salt
⅛ tsp. black pepper
1 to 2 Tbsp. olive oil
1 Tbsp. butter
4 slices bacon
1¼ cups coarsely shredded zucchini
½ cup chopped red onion
4 eggs, lightly beaten
1 cup half-and-half or light cream
¼ tsp. crushed red pepper
1 cup shredded Swiss cheese (4 oz.)
1 Tbsp. all-purpose flour

1. Preheat oven to 325°F. Peel and coarsely shred potatoes. Place potatoes in a large bowl; add enough water to cover. Stir well. Drain in a colander set in the sink. Repeat rinsing and draining two or three times until water runs clear. Drain again, pressing out as much water as you can with a spatula. Line a salad spinner with paper towels; add potatoes and spin. Repeat, if necessary, until potatoes are dry. (Or dry potatoes by patting them dry with paper towels.) Transfer potatoes to a large bowl. Sprinkle with ¼ teaspoon salt and the black pepper; toss to combine.

2. In a 12-inch nonstick skillet heat 1 tablespoon oil and the butter over medium-high until butter foams. Add potatoes, spreading in an even layer. Press gently with the back of a spatula to form a potato cake. Reduce heat to medium. Cook, without stirring, 12 minutes or until bottom is golden and crisp.

3. Place a baking sheet or cutting board over top of skillet. Carefully invert skillet to transfer potatoes to baking sheet. If necessary, add the remaining 1 tablespoon oil to skillet. Using the baking sheet, slide potatoes back into skillet. Cook 8 minutes more or until bottom is golden.

4. Lightly grease a 9-inch pie pan or plate. Use the baking sheet to transfer potato cake to pie pan; press potatoes into the bottom and up the sides of the pan.

5. In a large skillet cook bacon over medium until crisp. Remove bacon and drain on paper towels, reserving 1 tablespoon drippings in skillet. Crumble bacon; set aside. Add zucchini and onion to the reserved drippings. Cook over medium 3 to 5 minutes or until tender, stirring occasionally.

6. In a large bowl combine eggs, half-and-half, crushed red pepper, and remaining ¼ teaspoon salt. Stir in bacon and zucchini mixture. In a small bowl toss together cheese and flour; stir into egg mixture.

7. Pour egg mixture into the potato-lined pie pan. Bake, uncovered, 50 to 55 minutes or until a knife inserted near center comes out clean. Let stand 10 minutes before serving. Makes 8 servings.

PER SERVING *324 cal., 22 g fat (9 g sat. fat), 133 mg chol., 412 mg sodium, 20 g carb., 3 g fiber, 2 g sugars, 12 g pro.*

HASH-BROWN-CRUSTED QUICHE

GOLDEN MILK LATTE

GOLDEN MILK LATTE

PREP 5 minutes
SLOW COOK 2 hours (low)

6   cups refrigerated unsweetened
    coconut milk
2   Tbsp. honey
4   tsp. ground turmeric
2   tsp. ground ginger
1   tsp. ground cinnamon
    Dash ground cloves
    Dash black pepper
1   Tbsp. vanilla

1. In a 3½- or 4-quart slow cooker whisk together milk, honey, turmeric, ginger, cinnamon, cloves, and pepper.
2. Cover and cook on low 2 hours, whisking occasionally.
3. Add vanilla and whisk vigorously to froth before serving. If desired, lightly sprinkle each serving with additional ground cinnamon and sweeten with additional honey. Makes 12 servings.
PER SERVING *43 cal., 2 g fat (2 g sat. fat), 0 mg chol., 8 mg sodium, 5 g carb., 1 g fiber, 3 g sugars, 0 g pro.*

HOT CHOCOLATE TRUFFLES WITH MARSHMALLOWS

PREP 25 minutes
FREEZE 5 minutes

1   to 2 Tbsp. instant hot chocolate
    mix
1   to 2 Tbsp. marshmallow bits
1   to 2 Tbsp. mini chocolate chips or
    mint-chocolate chips
4   oz. semisweet or dark chocolate,
    chopped
    Melted white baking chocolate
    and/or sprinkles (optional)

1. For filling, in a small bowl combine hot chocolate mix, marshmallow bits, and chocolate chips.
2. Place 3 ounces of the chopped chocolate in a small microwave-safe bowl. Microwave 60 seconds or until melted, stirring every 15 seconds (temperature of melted chocolate should be 113°F). If necessary, microwave at 5- to 10-second intervals or until a thermometer registers 113°F. Add the remaining 1 ounce chopped chocolate. Stir vigorously 2 minutes or until completely smooth. If small pieces of chocolate remain, microwave at 5-second intervals, stirring until smooth. The chocolate temperature should be 88°F.
3. Use a small clean paintbrush to brush chocolate inside 1- to 2½-inch shallow silicone half-moon chocolate molds, creating a thick enough layer to coat sides completely.* Freeze 5 minutes.
4. Fill half the chocolate shells with 1 to 2 tablespoons filling. Carefully loosen and pop the remaining half of the chocolate shells from the molds. To assemble each chocolate truffle, brush edge of a filled chocolate shell (still in the mold) with some remaining melted chocolate; gently press edge of unfilled chocolate shell in melted chocolate to seal. Chill 2 to 3 minutes or until set. Carefully loosen and pop the assembled chocolate truffles from molds.
5. Place melted white chocolate in a resealable plastic bag. Snip a small hole in one corner. Drizzle white chocolate over tops of truffles; add sprinkles or other decoration. Freeze 5 minutes. Transfer truffles to a storage container. Store at room temperature up to 2 weeks.
6. To serve, place one truffle in a small mug for small truffles or a large mug for large truffles. Slowly pour 4 to 6 ounces simmered hot chocolate or milk over the truffle. Stir. Makes 6 servings.
*Tip The chocolate will set quickly in the molds. It's okay to brush over the chocolate that has set to ensure the molds are completely covered. Make a few at a time to determine the amount of chocolate that works best with the mold. Or brush a layer of chocolate, chill, and brush again.
PER SERVING *55 cal., 3 g fat (2 g sat. fat), 0 mg chol., 8 mg sodium, 8 g carb., 1 g fiber, 6 g sugars, 0 g pro.*

HOT CHOCOLATE
TRUFFLES WITH
MARSHMALLOWS

Fragrant Breads

Few aromas are as welcoming as bread baking in the oven. This collection features sweet pull-apart breads, yeasted rolls, donuts, tender popovers, and crisp crackers.

SPICED CIDER
DONUTS, PAGE 72

SNICKERDOODLE
CINNAMON KNOTS,
PAGE 64

CHEDDAR-CORNMEAL ROLLS

PREP 45 minutes
RISE 2 hours 15 minutes
BAKE 15 minutes at 375°F

4   to 4½ cups all-purpose flour
¾   cup cornmeal
2   pkg. active dry yeast
1¼   cups buttermilk or sour milk*
¼   cup sugar
3   Tbsp. butter or vegetable oil
3   Tbsp. Dijon mustard
1   tsp. salt
1   cup shredded sharp cheddar
     cheese (4 oz.)
2   eggs
1   recipe Roasted Red Pepper Butter
     (optional)

1. In a large bowl combine 1½ cups flour, the cornmeal, and yeast; set aside. In a small saucepan combine buttermilk, sugar, butter, mustard, and salt. Heat and stir just until warm (120°F to 130°F). Add buttermilk mixture, cheese, and eggs to flour mixture.

2. Beat with a mixer on low to medium 30 seconds, scraping sides of bowl constantly. Beat on high 3 minutes. Stir in as much remaining flour as you can.

3. Turn dough out onto a lightly floured surface. Knead in enough of the remaining flour to make a moderately stiff dough that is smooth and elastic (6 to 8 minutes total). Shape into a ball. Place dough in a large lightly greased bowl, turning once to grease surface. Cover; let rise in a warm place until double in size (about 1½ hours).

4. Punch dough down. Turn dough out onto a lightly floured surface. Divide dough in half. Cover; let rest for 10 minutes. Meanwhile, lightly grease twenty-four 2½-inch muffin cups.

5. Divide each dough half into 36 portions. Shape each portion into a ball, pulling edges under to make a smooth top. Place three balls, smooth sides up, in each prepared muffin cup. Cover muffin pans. Let rise in a warm place until nearly double in size (about 45 minutes).

6. Preheat oven to 375°F. Bake 15 minutes or until rolls sound hollow when lightly tapped. Immediately remove from muffin cups; cool slightly on wire racks. Serve warm. If desired, serve with Roasted Red Pepper Butter. Makes 24 servings.

CHEDDAR-CORNMEAL ROLLS

*Tip To make 1¼ cups sour milk, place
4 teaspoons lemon juice or vinegar in
a glass measuring cup. Add enough
milk to equal 1¼ cups total liquid; stir. Let
stand 5 minutes before using.

PER SERVING *149 cal., 4 g fat (2 g sat. fat),
27 mg chol., 199 mg sodium, 22 g carb.,
1 g fiber, 3 g sugars, 5 g pro.*

Roasted Red Pepper Butter Drain
¼ cup chopped bottled roasted red
sweet peppers; pat dry with paper
towels. In a food processor combine
the chopped peppers; ½ cup butter,
cut up and softened; and 1 clove
garlic, minced. Cover and process until
combined.

BUTTERMILK-SAGE DINNER ROLLS

PREP 45 minutes
RISE 1 hour
BAKE 15 minutes at 375°F

8	Tbsp. (1 stick) butter, cut up
10	fresh sage leaves, chopped
3	Tbsp. sugar
1½	cups buttermilk
2	pkg. active dry yeast
½	cup warm water (105°F to 115°F)
4½	cups all-purpose flour
2	tsp. kosher salt
½	tsp. baking soda
2	Tbsp. unsalted butter, melted

1. Lightly grease twenty-four
2½-inch muffin cups; set aside. In a
saucepan combine the cut-up butter,
sage, and 2 tablespoons sugar. Heat
and stir over medium-high just until
butter is melted. Stir in buttermilk and
heat just until warmed (do not boil).
Remove from heat; cool to room
temperature.
2. In a small bowl combine yeast and
remaining 1 tablespoon sugar. Stir in
warm water; let stand 5 minutes or
until yeast foams. Add yeast mixture to
buttermilk mixture; stir to combine.
3. In a another large bowl stir
together flour, salt, and baking soda.
Add buttermilk-yeast mixture. Stir to
combine, forming a sticky dough.
Loosely cover the bowl; let stand in a
warm place until dough has risen slightly
(about 30 minutes).
4. Turn dough out onto a lightly floured
surface. Knead several times or until
dough is easy to handle. Pinch off
pieces of dough and form into 1-inch

BUTTERMILK-SAGE
DINNER ROLLS

balls. To shape cloverleaf rolls, place
three 1-inch balls in each prepared
muffin cup. Loosely cover rolls with a
clean cloth and let rise in a warm place
until double in size (30 to 45 minutes).
5. Preheat oven to 375°F. Uncover
rolls. Brush lightly with melted butter.

Bake 15 minutes or until golden brown.
Remove rolls from muffin cups. Serve
warm. Makes 24 servings.
PER SERVING *142 cal., 5 g fat (3 g sat. fat),
13 mg chol., 205 mg sodium, 20 g carb.,
1 g fiber, 2 g sugars, 3 g pro.*

⅓	cup butter
⅓	cup granulated sugar
1	tsp. salt
2	eggs
½	cup packed brown sugar
2	Tbsp. ground cinnamon
½	cup melted butter
½	cup granulated sugar
¼	cup butter, softened

1. In a large bowl stir together 1½ cups flour and the yeast. In a 2-quart saucepan heat and stir next five ingredients (through salt) just until warm (120°F to 130°F) and butter is almost melted. Add milk mixture and eggs to flour mixture. Stir until combined. Stir in as much remaining flour as you can.
2. Turn dough out onto a lightly floured surface. Knead in enough remaining flour to make a moderately soft dough that is smooth and elastic (3 to 5 minutes total). Shape dough into a ball. Place in a lightly greased bowl, turning to grease surface of dough. Cover and let rise in a warm place until double in size (45 to 60 minutes).
3. Punch dough down. Turn out onto a floured surface. Divide dough in half. Cover and let rest 10 minutes. Meanwhile, line 2 large baking sheets with parchment paper. For filling, in a small bowl stir together brown sugar and 1 tablespoon cinnamon. Place melted butter in a small bowl. In another small bowl combine the ½ cup granulated sugar and remaining 1 tablespoon cinnamon.
4. Roll each half of dough to a 12×10-inch rectangle. Spread each half with 2 tablespoons softened butter and sprinkle each with half the filling. Fold each rectangle into thirds crosswise, then roll again into a 12×8-inch rectangle. Cut each rectangle lengthwise into 1-inch strips. Twist each strip several times, then tie each into a loose knot. Tuck ends into center of knot. Dip each knot into melted butter, then into granulated sugar-cinnamon mixture to coat. Arrange on prepared baking sheets. Cover and let rise in a warm place until nearly double (30 minutes).
5. Preheat oven to 375°F. Bake 18 to 20 minutes or until golden. Serve warm. Makes 16 servings.
PER SERVING *327 cal., 14 g fat (8 g sat. fat), 57 mg chol., 264 mg sodium, 46 g carb., 2 g fiber, 18 g sugars, 5 g pro.*

CHIVE BATTER ROLLS

PREP 30 minutes
RISE 30 minutes
BAKE 18 minutes at 350°F
COOL 5 minutes

1	Tbsp. yellow cornmeal
2	cups all-purpose flour
1	pkg. fast-rising active dry yeast
¼	tsp. black pepper
1	cup milk
3	Tbsp. butter
2	Tbsp. sugar
½	tsp. salt
1	egg
½	cup snipped fresh chives or ¼ cup finely chopped green onions (green tops only)
⅓	cup yellow cornmeal

1. Grease bottom and sides of twelve 2½-inch muffin cups. Sprinkle bottoms of cups with 1 tablespoon cornmeal. In a large bowl stir together 1¼ cups flour, the yeast, and pepper.
2. In a small saucepan combine milk, butter, sugar, and salt; heat and stir over medium just until mixture is warm (120°F to 130°F) and butter is almost melted. Add milk mixture and egg to flour mixture. Beat with a mixer on low to medium 30 seconds, scraping bowl constantly. Beat on high 3 minutes. Stir in chives and ⅓ cup cornmeal. Stir in remaining flour. (Batter will be soft and sticky.) Cover and let rest in a warm place 10 minutes.
3. Preheat oven to 350°F. Spoon batter into prepared muffin cups. Cover loosely. Let rise in a warm place 20 minutes.
4. Bake, uncovered, 18 minutes or until rolls sound hollow when tapped. Cool in muffin cups 5 minutes. Loosen edges and remove. Serve warm. Makes 12 servings.
PER SERVING *145 cal., 4 g fat (2 g sat. fat), 25 mg chol., 136 mg sodium, 23 g carb., 1 g fiber, 3 g sugars, 4 g pro.*

SNICKERDOODLE CINNAMON KNOTS

PREP 30 minutes
RISE 1 hour 15 minutes
BAKE 18 minutes at 375°F
COOL 5 minutes

4¼ to 4¾	cups all-purpose flour
1	pkg. active dry yeast
1	cup milk
1	cup mashed potato (tip, page 42)

SNICKERDOODLE
CINNAMON KNOTS

MAPLE-PEAR PULL-APART BREAD

MAPLE-APPLE PULL-APART BREAD

PREP 25 minutes
STAND 50 minutes
RISE 1 hour 25 minutes
BAKE 45 minutes at 350°F
COOL 10 minutes

¾ cup milk
1 pkg. active dry yeast
1 egg, lightly beaten
½ cup butter, melted
4 to 5 Tbsp. maple syrup
½ tsp. salt
3 cups all-purpose flour
1½ cups peeled, cored, finely chopped apples
¾ cup packed brown sugar
1 tsp. ground cardamom
¾ cup powdered sugar

1. In a small saucepan heat milk until warm (105°F to 115°F). In a large bowl combine warm milk and yeast; stir until yeast is dissolved. Let stand 5 minutes.
2. Add egg, ¼ cup melted butter, 2 tablespoons maple syrup, and the salt to yeast mixture. Beat with a mixer on medium until combined. Add half the flour; beat on low 30 seconds, scraping bowl as needed. Beat 1 minute on medium. Stir in remaining flour. Shape dough into a ball (dough will not be smooth). Place in a greased bowl; turn once to grease surface. Cover; let rise in a warm place until nearly double in size (45 to 60 minutes).
3. Grease a 9×5-inch loaf pan. Turn dough out onto a lightly floured surface. Roll dough into a 20×12-inch rectangle. Brush dough with the remaining ¼ cup melted butter.
4. Sprinkle dough with apples, brown sugar, and cardamom. Cut rectangle in half lengthwise to make two 20×6-inch strips. Cut each strip crosswise into five 6×4-inch strips. Make two stacks of five strips each. Cut each stack into three 4×2-inch sections. Stagger sections in pan, cut sides up. Cover; let rise in a warm place until nearly double in size (40 to 45 minutes).
5. Meanwhile, preheat oven to 350°F. Bake 45 minutes or until golden brown and an instant read thermometer inserted near center registers 200°F. Cool in pan 10 minutes. Transfer to a serving plate. Stir together powdered sugar and 2 tablespoons maple syrup.

STRAWBERRY-BANANA BREAD

Add enough remaining maple syrup to make drizzling consistency. Drizzle over loaf. Makes 10 servings.
Make Ahead Prepare as directed through Step 2, except do not let dough rise. Cover bowl and refrigerate up to 24 hours. Let dough stand at room temperature 30 minutes before continuing with Step 3.
PER SERVING *370 cal., 11 g fat (6 g sat. fat), 44 mg chol., 212 mg sodium, 64 g carb., 2 g fiber, 33 g sugars, 6 g pro.*

STRAWBERRY-BANANA BREAD

PREP 25 minutes
BAKE 45 minutes at 350°F
COOL 10 minutes

2 cups all-purpose flour
1½ tsp. baking powder
½ tsp. baking soda
½ tsp. ground cinnamon
¼ tsp. salt
¼ tsp. ground nutmeg
⅛ tsp. ground ginger
2 eggs, lightly beaten

1 cup mashed banana
½ cup sliced strawberries
1 cup sugar
½ cup vegetable oil
¼ cup chopped walnuts (optional)

1. Preheat oven to 350°F. Grease bottom and ½ inch up the sides of a 9×5-inch loaf pan; set aside. In a large bowl combine flour, baking powder, baking soda, cinnamon, salt, nutmeg, and ginger. Make a well in the center of flour mixture; set aside.
2. In a medium bowl combine eggs, banana, strawberries, sugar, and oil. Add egg mixture all at once to flour mixture. Stir just until moistened. Fold in nuts, if using. Spoon batter into prepared pan.
3. Bake 45 minutes or until a toothpick inserted near center comes out clean. Cool in pan on a wire rack 10 minutes. Remove from pan; cool completely on a wire rack. Makes 16 servings.
PER SERVING *196 cal., 8 g fat (1 g sat. fat), 23 mg chol., 131 mg sodium, 30 g carb., 1 g fiber, 16 g sugars, 3 g pro.*

FRESH CRANBERRY-PEPITA BUTTERMILK BREAD

PREP 20 minutes
BAKE 55 minutes at 375°F
COOL 10 minutes

2   cups all-purpose flour
1   cup sugar
2½   tsp. baking powder
¼   tsp. baking soda
¼   tsp. salt
2   eggs, lightly beaten
1   cup buttermilk
6   Tbsp. butter, melted
1¼   cups fresh or frozen cranberries
¾   cup salted, roasted pepitas or pistachios
2   tsp. tangerine or orange zest

1. Preheat oven to 375°F. Grease an 8×4-inch loaf pan. In a large bowl stir together flour, ¾ cup sugar, the baking powder, baking soda, and salt. Make a well in center of flour mixture.
2. In a medium bowl whisk together eggs, buttermilk, and melted butter. Add egg mixture all at once to flour mixture. Stir just until moistened (batter should be lumpy). Fold in cranberries, ½ cup of the pepitas, and tangerine zest.
3. Spoon batter into prepared loaf pan. Coarsely chop the remaining ¼ cup pepitas. In a small bowl combine the chopped pepitas and remaining ¼ cup sugar; sprinkle evenly over batter.
4. Bake 55 minutes or until a toothpick inserted in center comes out clean. Cover with foil the last 5 to 10 minutes of baking to prevent overbrowning, if necessary. Cool in pan on a wire rack 10 minutes. Remove from pan; cool completely on wire rack. Makes 10 servings.

PER SERVING 316 cal., 13 g fat (6 g sat. fat), 57 mg chol., 358 mg sodium, 44 g carb., 2 g fiber, 22 g sugars, 8 g pro.

DOUBLE-CHOCOLATE S'MORES BANANA BREAD

PREP 15 minutes
BAKE 1 hour at 350°F
COOL 10 minutes

1½   cups all-purpose flour
½   cup unsweetened cocoa powder
1   tsp. baking powder
½   tsp. baking soda
½   tsp. salt
2   eggs, lightly beaten
1½   cups mashed bananas
½   cup granulated sugar
½   cup packed brown sugar
½   cup vegetable oil
1   tsp. vanilla
1   cup milk chocolate chips
1   cup coarsely crushed graham crackers
1   cup vanilla marshmallow bits (such as Kraft Mallow Bits)

1. Preheat oven to 350°F. Grease a 9×5-inch loaf pan. In a large bowl combine flour, cocoa powder, baking powder, baking soda, and salt. Make a well in center of flour mixture.
2. In a medium bowl combine the eggs, bananas, sugars, oil, and vanilla. Add egg mixture all at once to flour mixture. Stir just until moistened. Fold in ¾ cup chocolate chips, ¾ cup graham crackers, and ¾ cup marshmallow bits. Transfer batter to prepared pan. In a small bowl combine remaining ¼ cup each chocolate chips, graham crackers, and marshmallow bits; sprinkle over batter.
3. Bake 1 hour or until a toothpick inserted in center comes out clean. Cover with foil the last 10 minutes of baking to prevent overbrowning, if necessary. Cool in pan on a wire rack 10 minutes. Remove from pan; cool completely on wire rack. Makes 8 servings.

PER SERVING 596 cal., 26 g fat (9 g sat. fat), 57 mg chol., 383 mg sodium, 92 g carb., 6 g fiber, 56 g sugars, 8 g pro.

FRESH CRANBERRY-PEPITA BUTTERMILK BREAD

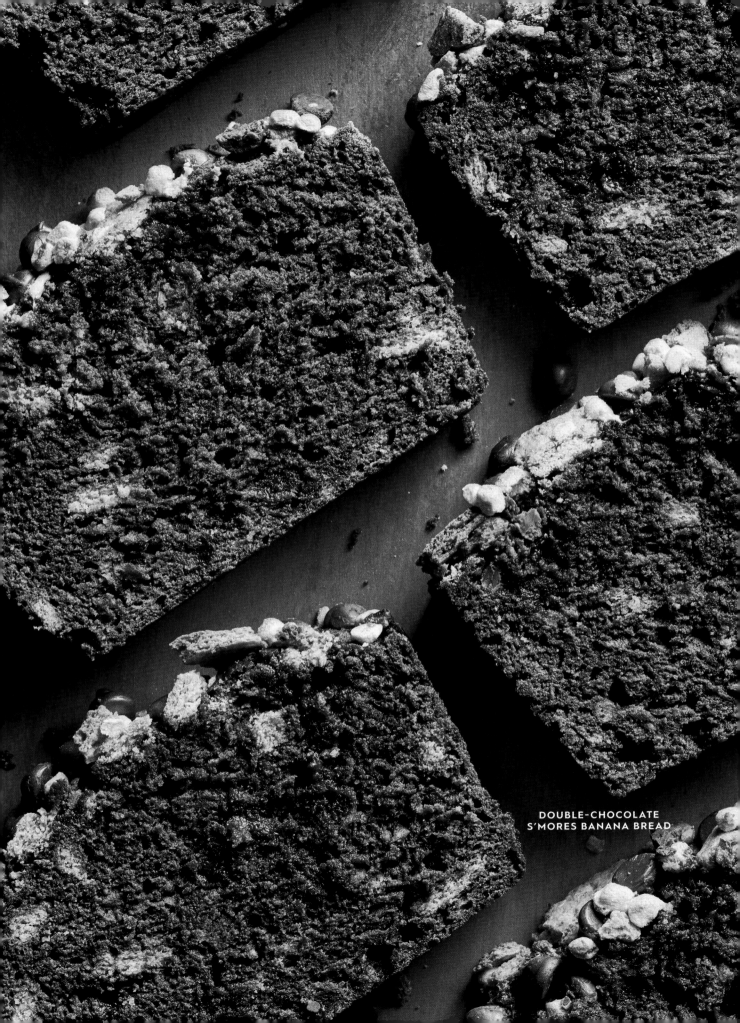

DOUBLE-CHOCOLATE
S'MORES BANANA BREAD

APPLE FRITTER
BREAD

APPLE FRITTER BREAD

PREP 20 minutes
BAKE 1 hour at 350°F
COOL 10 minutes

1   tart cooking apple, such as
     Granny Smith, peeled, cored, and
     finely chopped (1¼ cups)
¼   cup packed brown sugar
1   tsp. ground cinnamon
1½   cups all-purpose flour
2   tsp. baking powder
¼   tsp. salt
1   cup granulated sugar
⅓   cup butter, softened
2   eggs, lightly beaten
½   cup milk
1   tsp. vanilla
1   recipe Sour Cream Icing

1. Preheat oven to 350°F. Grease an 8×4-inch loaf pan. In a medium bowl combine apple, brown sugar, and cinnamon. In another medium bowl combine flour, baking powder, and salt.
2. In large bowl beat sugar and butter until combined. One at a time, beat in eggs. Beat in milk and vanilla. Add flour mixture; stir just until combined. Pour half the batter into the prepared loaf pan. Add half the apple mixture. Spread remaining batter over apples in pan. Top with remaining apple mixture. Lightly pat apples into batter. Use a table knife to swirl apples into batter.
3. Bake 1 hour or until a toothpick inserted in center comes out clean. Cover with foil the last 10 minutes to prevent overbrowning, if necessary.

Cool in pan on a wire rack 10 minutes. Remove from pan; cool completely on a wire rack. Drizzle with Sour Cream Icing before slicing and serving. Makes 10 servings.

Sour Cream Icing In a small bowl combine 3 tablespoons sour cream, ½ teaspoon vanilla, and ¾ cup powdered sugar. If necessary, beat in enough milk, 1 teaspoon at a time, until drizzling consistency.

PER SERVING *294 cal., 8 g fat (5 g sat. fat), 56 mg chol., 227 mg sodium, 52 g carb., 1 g fiber, 37 g sugars, 4 g pro.*

HUMMINGBIRD BREAD

PREP 20 minutes
BAKE 1 hour at 350°F
COOL 10 minutes

2   cups all-purpose flour
2   tsp. baking powder
1   tsp. ground cinnamon
½   tsp. baking soda
½   tsp. salt
¼   tsp. ground allspice
1   8-oz. can crushed pineapple,
    drained
1   cup mashed overripe bananas
1   cup sugar
½   cup vegetable oil
2   eggs, lightly beaten
1   tsp. vanilla
½   cup shredded or flaked coconut
¼   cup chopped toasted pecans (tip,
    page 24)
1   recipe Cream Cheese Drizzle

1. Preheat oven to 350°F. Grease the bottom and ½ inch up the sides of a 9×5-inch loaf pan. In a large bowl stir together the flour, baking powder, cinnamon, baking soda, salt, and allspice. Make a well in center of flour mixture.
2. In a medium bowl combine pineapple, bananas, sugar, oil, eggs, and vanilla. Add pineapple mixture all at once to flour mixture. Stir just until moistened. Fold in coconut and pecans. Transfer batter to prepared loaf pan.
3. Bake 1 hour or until a toothpick inserted in center comes out clean. Cool in pan on a wire rack 10 minutes. Remove from pan; cool completely. Drizzle with Cream Cheese Drizzle. If desired, sprinkle with additional coconut and pecans. Makes 10 servings.
Cream Cheese Drizzle In a small bowl combine 1 ounce cream cheese, softened, and 1 tablespoon butter, softened, until smooth. Stir in ½ cup powdered sugar and enough milk (about 1 tablespoon) to reach drizzling consistency.
PER SERVING *388 cal., 18 g fat (4 g sat. fat), 43 mg chol., 312 mg sodium, 55 g carb., 2 g fiber, 31 g sugars, 5 g pro.*

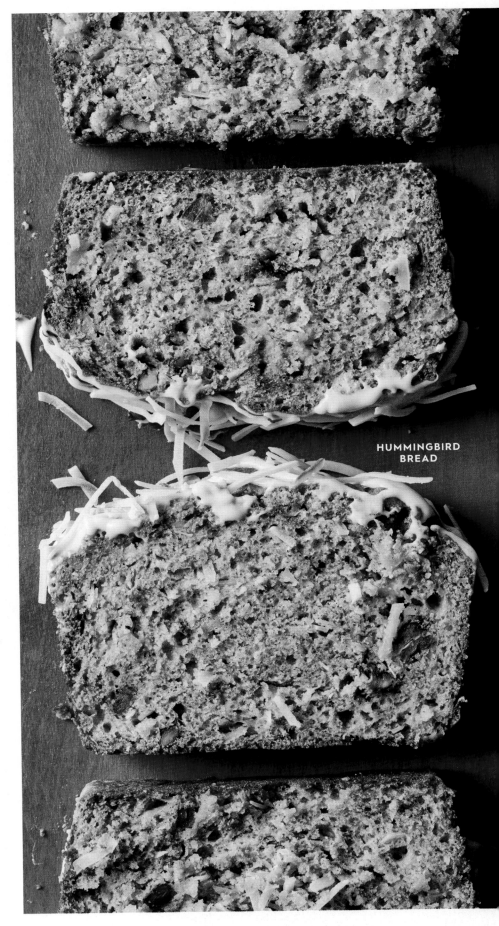

HUMMINGBIRD
BREAD

CARROT CAKE QUICK BREAD

PREP 25 minutes
BAKE 55 minutes at 350°F
COOL 1 hour

- 1½ cups all-purpose flour
- 1 tsp. baking powder
- ½ tsp. salt
- ½ tsp. ground cinnamon
- ¼ tsp. baking soda
- 2 eggs, lightly beaten
- 1½ cups lightly packed, finely shredded carrots
- ¾ cup vegetable oil
- ½ cup granulated sugar
- ½ cup packed brown sugar
- 1 tsp. vanilla
- 1 cup chopped candied, glazed, or toasted pecans
- 2 Tbsp. quick-cooking rolled oats
- 1 Tbsp. sweetened shredded coconut
- 1 Tbsp. melted butter

1. Preheat oven to 350°F. Grease bottom and ½ inch up sides of an 8×4-inch loaf pan. In a large bowl stir together first five ingredients (through baking soda). Make a well in center of flour mixture.

2. In a medium bowl combine the next six ingredients (through vanilla). Add carrot mixture all at once to flour mixture. Stir just until moistened (batter should be lumpy). Fold in ½ cup candied pecans. Spread batter into prepared pan. For streusel, in a small bowl combine remaining ½ cup candied pecans, the oats, coconut, and butter. Sprinkle over batter.

3. Bake 55 to 60 minutes or until a toothpick inserted in center comes out clean. Cover loaf with foil the last 10 minutes of baking to prevent overbrowning, if necessary. Cool in pan on a wire rack 10 minutes. Remove from pan; cool on wire rack. Wrap and store overnight before slicing. Makes 12 servings.

PER SERVING *328 cal., 20 g fat (3 g sat. fat), 34 mg chol., 231 mg sodium, 35 g carb., 1 g fiber, 22 g sugars, 3 g pro.*

SPICED CIDER DONUTS

PREP 45 minutes
RISE 1 hour 45 minutes
FRY 2 minutes per batch

- 3¼ to 3¾ cups all-purpose flour
- 2 pkg. active dry yeast (4½ tsp.)
- 1½ tsp. ancho chile powder or ground cardamom
- ¾ cup peeled, cored, and finely chopped apple
- ½ cup butter
- ½ cup apple cider or apple juice
- ¼ cup milk
- ¼ cup sugar
- 1 tsp. salt
- 2 eggs, lightly beaten
  Vegetable oil for deep-fat frying
- 1 recipe Spiced Glaze

1. In a large bowl stir together 1¾ cups flour, the yeast, and chile powder. In a medium saucepan heat and stir the next six ingredients (through salt) just until warm (120°F to 130°F) and butter is almost melted. Add cider mixture and eggs to flour mixture; stir to combine. Stir in as much remaining flour as you can.

2. Turn dough out onto a lightly floured surface. Knead in enough remaining flour to make a moderately soft dough that is smooth and elastic (3 to 5 minutes). Shape into a ball. Place in a lightly greased bowl, turning once to grease surface. Cover; let rise in a warm place until double in size (1 to 1½ hours).

3. Punch dough down. Turn out onto a lightly floured surface. Divide in half. Cover; let rest 10 minutes. Line a large baking sheet with parchment paper. Lightly flour parchment.

4. Roll each dough half to ½-inch thickness. Cut dough with a floured 2½-inch donut cutter, dipping cutter in flour between cuts. Reroll scraps as necessary. Place donuts and donut holes on prepared baking sheet. Cover with a light kitchen towel; let rise in a warm place until double in size (45 to 60 minutes).

5. In a heavy 3-quart saucepan heat 1½ inches oil over medium to 365°F.* (If using an electric deep-fat fryer, follow manufacturer's directions.) Fry donuts and holes in batches, two or three at a time, for 2 minutes or until golden brown, turning once. (To prevent donuts from absorbing too much oil, use a deep-fry thermometer to maintain oil temperature at 365°F.) Use a slotted spoon to transfer donuts to paper towels to drain.*

6. Dip tops of donuts and holes in Spiced Glaze. Let stand until glaze is set. Makes 21 servings.

***Tip** Alternatively, bake at 350°F 12 to 15 minutes, or lightly coat with vegetable oil spray and air-fry 4 to 5 minutes.

Spiced Glaze In a small bowl combine 2 cups powdered sugar and ¼ teaspoon ancho chile powder or ground cardamom. Stir in enough milk (2 to 3 tablespoons) for a thin icing.

PER SERVING *319 cal., 21 g fat (5 g sat. fat), 30 mg chol., 156 mg sodium, 31 g carb., 1 g fiber, 15 g sugars, 3 g pro.*

CARROT CAKE QUICK BREAD

SPICED CIDER
DONUTS

SALT-AND-PEPPER
CRACKERS

FENNEL SEED
WINE CRACKERS

SAGE AND PEPPER POPOVERS

PREP 15 minutes
BAKE 40 minutes at 400°F

1   Tbsp. shortening or nonstick
    cooking spray
2   eggs, lightly beaten
1   cup milk
1   Tbsp. olive oil
1   cup all-purpose flour
2   Tbsp. grated Parmesan cheese
2   tsp. finely snipped fresh sage or
    thyme or ½ teaspoon dried sage
    or thyme, crushed
½   tsp. salt
½   tsp. freshly ground black pepper

1. Preheat oven to 400°F. Using
½ teaspoon shortening for each cup,
grease the bottoms and sides of six
popover cups or 6-ounce custard cups.
(Or lightly coat with cooking spray.)
If using custard cups, place cups in a
15×10-inch baking pan; set aside.
2. In a medium bowl combine eggs,
milk, and oil. Stir in flour until smooth. Stir
in cheese, sage, salt, and pepper.
3. Fill prepared cups half full with batter.
Bake 40 minutes or until very firm.
4. Immediately after removing from
oven, prick each popover with a fork
to let steam escape. Turn off oven. For
crisper popovers, return to oven for
5 to 10 minutes or until popovers reach
desired crispness. Remove popovers
from cups. Serve immediately. Makes
6 servings.
PER SERVING *153 cal., 7 g fat (2 g sat. fat),
74 mg chol., 237 mg sodium, 17 g carb.,
1 g fiber, 0 g sugars, 5 g pro.*

FENNEL SEED WINE CRACKERS

PREP 20 minutes
BAKE 18 minutes at 325°F

1   cup all-purpose flour
2   tsp. fennel seeds, crushed
½   tsp. salt
⅛   tsp. black pepper
3   Tbsp. dry white wine
3   Tbsp. olive oil
    Coarse kosher salt (optional)

1. Preheat oven to 325°F. In a bowl
combine flour, fennel seeds, salt, and
pepper. In another bowl combine wine
and olive oil; gradually add to dry

SAGE AND PEPPER POPOVERS

ingredients, tossing with a fork until
combined. Form dough into a ball.
2. On a lightly floured surface, roll
dough into a 12×9-inch rectangle, about
¹⁄₁₆-inch thickness (trim uneven edges,
if necessary). Using a fork, prick dough
all over. Using a pastry wheel or knife,
cut into 3×1½-inch rectangles. Transfer
rectangles to an ungreased baking
sheet. If desired, sprinkle lightly with
kosher salt.
3. Bake 18 minutes or just until crackers
start to brown and are firm to the touch.
Cool completely on wire racks. Makes
24 servings.
Food Processor Method In a food
processor combine flour, fennel seeds,
salt, and pepper; cover and process just
until combined. Add wine and olive oil.
Cover and process just until combined.
Form dough into a ball. Continue as
directed in Step 2.
PER SERVING *36 cal., 2 g fat (0 g sat. fat),
0 mg chol., 49 mg sodium, 4 g carb.,
0 g fiber, 0 g sugars, 1 g pro.*

SALT-AND-PEPPER CRACKERS

PREP 25 minutes
BAKE 15 minutes at 375°F

1¾ cups all-purpose flour
¾   cup corn tortilla flour or corn flour
1   Tbsp. sugar
½   tsp. baking soda
2¼ tsp. kosher salt

2   Tbsp. butter
1   cup buttermilk
    Water
3   to 4 freshly cracked dried green
    whole peppercorns, peppercorn
    mix, or black whole peppercorns

1. Preheat oven to 375°F. Line a baking
sheet with parchment paper. In a large
bowl stir together the flours, sugar,
baking soda, and ¼ teaspoon salt.
Using a pastry blender, cut in butter
until mixture resembles coarse crumbs.
Make a well in center of flour mixture.
Add buttermilk. Using a fork, stir until
mixture can be shaped into a ball.
2. Turn dough out onto a lightly floured
surface. Knead 8 to 10 strokes or until
dough is almost smooth. Divide dough
into 6 portions. Roll each portion into a
9×6-inch free-form rectangle (⅛-inch
thickness). Use a pastry wheel or knife
to cut rectangles into quarters. Using a
fork, prick rectangles well. Place 1 inch
apart on prepared baking sheet.
3. Lightly brush crackers with water.
Sprinkle with peppercorns and the
remaining 2 teaspoons salt; press into
dough. Bake 15 minutes or until crisp.
Transfer to wire racks; cool completely.
Store in an airtight container at room
temperature up to 1 week. Makes
24 servings.
PER SERVING *59 cal., 1 g fat (1 g sat. fat),
3 mg chol., 247 mg sodium, 10 g carb.,
0 g fiber, 0 g sugars, 2 g pro.*

Just Desserts

Indulgent sweets are a great pleasure of the season. Choose from beautiful cakes, delicious pies, fruit-filled cobblers and crisps, and rich pots de crème.

CHAMPAGNE CAKE,
PAGE 80

CHERRY-PECAN
CRÈME BRÛLÉE,
PAGE 92

BLACK FOREST CAKE ROLL

PREP 35 minutes
STAND 30 minutes
BAKE 20 minutes at 325°F
COOL 1 hour
CHILL 1 hour 30 minutes

6   eggs
1   tsp. vanilla
¼   tsp. salt
1¼   cups powdered sugar
3   Tbsp. all-purpose flour
3   Tbsp. unsweetened Dutch-process
     cocoa powder
     Powdered sugar
⅓   cup granulated sugar
4   tsp. cornstarch
2   cups frozen unsweetened pitted
     tart red cherries

3   Tbsp. brandy or cranberry juice
2   inches stick cinnamon
1   Tbsp. cold water
½   tsp. unflavored gelatin
¾   cup whipping cream
2   Tbsp. granulated sugar
½   cup whipping cream
6   oz. chopped semisweet or
     bittersweet chocolate
2   Tbsp. chopped milk chocolate,
     melted
     Chocolate curls (optional)

1. Separate eggs. Allow egg whites and yolks to stand at room temperature 30 minutes. Meanwhile, grease the bottom of a 15×10-inch baking pan. Line bottom with waxed paper or parchment paper; grease and lightly flour pan. Set aside.

2. Preheat oven to 325°F. In a medium bowl beat egg yolks, vanilla, and salt with a mixer on high 4 to 5 minutes or until thick and lemon color. Gradually add 1¼ cups powdered sugar, beating until combined; set aside. Thoroughly wash beaters. In a large bowl beat egg whites on medium to high until stiff peaks form (tips stand straight). Fold about one-fourth of the beaten egg whites into egg yolk mixture; fold egg yolk mixture into remaining beaten egg whites. Sift flour and cocoa powder over egg mixture; fold in gently just until combined. Spread batter in prepared baking pan.

3. Bake 20 minutes or until cake springs back when lightly touched. Immediately loosen edges of cake from pan and turn cake out onto a clean kitchen towel sprinkled with additional powdered sugar. Remove waxed paper. Roll towel and cake into a spiral, starting from a short side of the cake. Cool on a wire rack.

4. Meanwhile, for brandied cherries, in a medium saucepan stir together ⅓ cup granulated sugar and the cornstarch. Stir in cherries, brandy, and stick cinnamon. Cook and stir over medium heat until thickened and bubbly. Cook and stir 2 minutes more. Transfer to a medium bowl; cool completely. Remove stick cinnamon.

5. For filling, in a 1-cup glass measuring cup combine the cold water and gelatin. Let stand 2 minutes. Place measuring cup in a small saucepan of boiling water. Cook and stir 1 minute or until gelatin is completely dissolved. Cool 5 minutes. In a large bowl beat ¾ cup whipping cream and 2 tablespoons granulated sugar on medium while drizzling with gelatin mixture. Continue beating cream mixture until stiff peaks form (tips stand straight).

6. Unroll cake; remove towel. Spread cake with filling to within 1 inch of edges. Spoon brandied cherries evenly over filling. Reroll cake from a short side, being careful to keep filling in place; trim ends. Place cake roll, seam side down, on a wire rack set over a baking sheet. Cover and chill 1 hour.

7. For ganache, in a small saucepan bring ½ cup whipping cream just to boiling over medium. Remove from heat. Add semisweet chocolate (do not stir).

**BLACK FOREST
CAKE ROLL**

Let stand 5 minutes. Stir until smooth. Cool 15 minutes or until thickened (if necessary, chill until thickened).

8. Fill a heavy resealable plastic bag with melted milk chocolate; set aside. Spread ganache over top and sides of cake roll. Snip a small hole in one corner of the bag of milk chocolate; pipe evenly spaced lines of chocolate across cake. Pull tip of a toothpick or fork across lines to create a scalloped pattern. Chill cake 30 minutes or until chocolate is set. Transfer to a serving platter. If desired, garnish with chocolate curls. Makes 10 servings.

PER SERVING 383 cal., 20 g fat (11 g sat. fat), 153 mg chol., 115 mg sodium, 44 g carb., 2 g fiber, 36 g sugars, 7 g pro.

MINIATURE ORANGE-CRANBERRY CAKES

PREP 1 hour
STAND 30 minutes
BAKE 20 minutes at 325°F
COOL 10 minutes

¾ cup butter
3 eggs
   Nonstick spray for baking
1½ cups all-purpose flour
1 tsp. baking powder
¼ tsp. ground nutmeg
¾ cup granulated sugar
¼ cup orange liqueur or orange juice
1 tsp. orange zest
½ tsp. vanilla
½ cup dried cranberries, finely snipped
⅓ cup granulated sugar
¼ cup water
2 Tbsp. packed brown sugar
2 Tbsp. light-color corn syrup
½ cup orange juice
   Orange peel curls and fresh cranberries (optional)

1. Allow butter and eggs to stand at room temperature 30 minutes. Meanwhile, preheat oven to 325°F. Generously coat six 4-inch fluted tube pans or one 6-cup fluted tube pan with baking spray; set aside. In a small bowl stir together flour, baking powder, and nutmeg; set aside.
2. In a large bowl beat butter with a mixer on medium to high 30 seconds. Gradually add the ¾ cup granulated sugar, beating on medium 5 minutes or until light and fluffy.

MINIATURE ORANGE-CRANBERRY CAKES

3. Stir in orange liqueur, orange zest, and vanilla. Add eggs, one at a time, beating on low to medium 1 minute after each addition and scraping sides of bowl frequently. Gradually add flour mixture, beating on low just until combined. Stir in dried cranberries.
4. Pour batter into prepared pans, spreading evenly. Bake 20 to 25 minutes for 4-inch pans (40 to 45 minutes for 6-cup pan) or until a toothpick inserted near centers comes out clean. Cool in pans on wire racks 10 minutes. Remove from pans; cool completely on racks. Generously prick tops and sides of cakes with a fork.
5. For syrup, in a medium saucepan combine the ⅓ cup granulated sugar, the water, brown sugar, and corn syrup.

Cook and stir over medium until bubbly and most of the sugar is dissolved. Remove from heat. Stir in orange juice; cool slightly.
6. Dip top and sides of each 4-inch cake into syrup; place on wire racks above a large tray or baking sheet. Spoon or brush remaining syrup over tops of cakes. (If using 6-cup pan, place cake on a wire rack over tray or baking sheet; spoon or brush syrup over top and side of cake, reusing syrup on tray or baking sheet.) Cool cakes. If desired, garnish with orange peel curls and/or cranberries. Makes 6 servings.
PER SERVING 591 cal., 26 g fat (15 g sat. fat), 167 mg chol., 264 mg sodium, 82 g carb., 2 g fiber, 50 g sugars, 7 g pro.

**PUMPKIN-SPICE
ICEBOX CAKE**

PUMPKIN-SPICE
ICEBOX CAKE

PREP 20 minutes
FREEZE 20 minutes
CHILL 1 hour

2   cups heavy cream
1   cup sifted powdered sugar
2   tsp. vanilla
1   tsp. ground nutmeg
½   cup canned pumpkin
¾   cup dulce de leche
2   5.25-oz. pkg. thin gingersnap
    cookies (40 cookies)*
    Ground cinnamon

1. In a large bowl beat cream, ½ cup powdered sugar, the vanilla, and nutmeg with a mixer on medium until stiff peaks form(tips stand straight). Fold in pumpkin and remaining ½ cup powdered sugar. Transfer mixture to a disposable piping bag or resealable plastic bag. Cut off the tip or corner of bag to pipe.

2. Spread a thin layer (about ½ teaspoon) dulce de leche on each gingersnap cookie, then pipe about 2 teaspoons cream mixture on top. Stack cookies together to make 4 stacks of 10 cookies. Lay the first cookie stack on its side at the end of an oval or rectangular platter (pipe a bit of

cream under it to hold it in place). Lay remaining stacks next to each other on the platter so they touch. Freeze 20 minutes.

3. Pipe the outsides of the stacks all over with remaining cream mixture, then spread evenly using a knife dipped in water to smooth and square edges. Loosely cover in plastic wrap (insert a few toothpicks in top to keep plastic from sticking to cake). Refrigerate at least 1 hour or up to overnight.

4. To serve, warm remaining dulce de leche in microwave, thinning with a little milk or cream if needed. Slice cake crosswise into eight slices (through the center of each cookie stack), cleaning the knife between each cut. Drizzle each slice with dulce de leche and sprinkle with cinnamon. Makes 8 servings.

*Or use regular gingersnaps and reduce to 32 cookies, using 8 cookies per stack.

PER SERVING *514 cal., 28 g fat (16 g sat. fat), 75 mg chol., 250 mg sodium, 61 g carb., 1 g fiber, 37 g sugars, 6 g pro.*

CHAMPAGNE CAKE

Photo, page 76
PREP 1 hour
STAND 30 minutes
BAKE 25 minutes at 350°F
COOL 10 minutes

¾   cup butter
6   egg whites
3   cups all-purpose flour, plus more
    for dusting
1   Tbsp. baking powder
1   tsp. salt
1½ cups sugar
2   tsp. vanilla
1½ cups champagne
1   recipe Champagne Butter Frosting
8   to 10 purchased gumballs
15 to 20 gold sixlets

1. Allow butter and egg whites to stand at room temperature 30 minutes. Meanwhile, grease three 8-inch round cake pans. Line bottom of pans with parchment paper. Grease paper and lightly flour pans; set aside. In a medium bowl stir together flour, baking powder, and salt; set aside.

2. Preheat oven to 350°F. In a large bowl beat butter with a mixer on medium to high 30 seconds. Add sugar

and vanilla. Beat on medium 3 minutes or until light and fluffy. Alternately add flour mixture and champagne to butter mixture, beating on low after each addition just until combined.

3. Wash beaters thoroughly. In a medium bowl beat egg whites on high until stiff peaks form (tips stand straight). Fold beaten egg whites into cake batter. Divide batter evenly among prepared pans.

4. Bake 25 to 30 minutes or until a wooden toothpick inserted in center of cakes comes out clean. Cool in pans on wire racks 10 minutes. Remove cakes from pans; remove parchment paper. Cool completely on wire racks.

5. If necessary to level bottom and middle layers, trim crowns of two layers with a serrated knife. Place one trimmed cake layer, bottom side down, on serving platter. Dust crumbs with a pastry brush. Spoon ¾ cup frosting in center of cake layer. With offset spatula, spread frosting just to edge of cake. Top with second layer, bottom side down. Spread with ¾ cup frosting in center of cake layer. With offset spatula, spread frosting just to edge of cake.

6. Place top layer on middle layer, crown-side up. Frost top and sides of cake with thin layer of frosting to seal crumbs. Frost sides of cake, using offset spatula to smooth frosting. Spoon remaining frosting on center top. With offset spatula, spread frosting to edges. Use spatula to smooth frosting and blend top with sides. Top cake with gumballs and sixlets. Makes 12 servings.

Champagne Butter Frosting In a large bowl beat 1½ cups softened butter with a mixer on medium to high 30 seconds. Gradually add 2 cups powdered sugar, beating well. Slowly beat in 4 to 5 tablespoons champagne, sparkling wine, or milk and 1 teaspoon vanilla. Gradually beat in 3 cups powdered sugar. Beat in enough additional champagne to reach spreading consistency.

PER SERVING *837 cal., 39 fat (25 g sat. fat), 93 mg chol., 626 mg sodium, 120 g carb., 1 g fiber, 90 g sugars, 6 g pro.*

WHITE CHRISTMAS
PEPPERMINT LAYER CAKE

WHITE CHRISTMAS PEPPERMINT LAYER CAKE

PREP 30 minutes
BAKE 30 minutes at 350°F
COOL 10 minutes

2¼ cups cake flour, plus more for
    dusting
1   Tbsp. baking powder
1¼ cups whole milk
4   egg whites
1   tsp. vanilla
½   cup butter, softened (1 stick)
1½ cups granulated sugar
¾   cup butter, softened (1½ sticks)
8   cups powdered sugar
⅓   cup milk
2   tsp. peppermint extract
    Red or pink food coloring
    Peppermint sticks, candy canes, or
    peppermint candies

1. Preheat oven to 350°F. For cake, grease two 8-inch round cake pans. Line bottoms with waxed paper; grease paper; lightly dust pans with flour.
2. In a medium bowl stir together flour and baking powder. In another medium bowl whisk together milk, egg whites, and vanilla.
3. In a large bowl beat ½ cup butter with a mixer on low to medium 30 seconds. Add granulated sugar; beat 3 minutes on medium. Alternately add flour and milk mixtures to butter mixture, beating on low after each addition just until combined. Beat 2 minutes on medium. Divide batter between prepared pans.
4. Bake 30 to 35 minutes or until a wooden toothpick inserted near centers comes out clean. Cool in pans on wire racks 10 minutes. Run a knife around sides of cakes; remove layers from pans. Peel off waxed paper. Invert cake layers and cool completely on racks.

5. Meanwhile, prepare frosting. In an extra-large bowl beat ¾ cup butter with a mixer on medium until smooth. Gradually add 2 cups powdered sugar, beating well. Slowly beat in ⅓ cup milk and peppermint extract. Gradually beat in remaining powdered sugar. Beat in additional milk, if needed, to reach spreading consistency. Transfer 2 cups frosting to a medium bowl. Add food coloring to make a delicate shade of pink; stir to thoroughly combine.
6. With a long, sharp serrated knife, split each cake horizontally to make four layers. Place one cake layer, cut side up, on a serving plate. Spread top of cake with ⅔ cup pink frosting. Repeat with two more cake layers and pink frosting. Top with the final cake layer, cut side down. Spread white frosting over top and sides of cake. Decorate with peppermint candies. Makes 12 servings.
PER SERVING *716 cal., 20 g fat (13 g sat. fat), 54 mg chol., 327 mg sodium, 131 g carb., 0 g fiber, 108 g sugars, 5 g pro.*

CARAMEL APPLE
POKE CAKE

CARAMEL APPLE POKE CAKE

PREP 25 minutes
BAKE 30 minutes at 350°F

- 2   cups all-purpose flour
- 2   tsp. baking powder
- ½   tsp. baking soda
- ½   tsp. salt
- ⅔   cup butter, softened
- 1   cup sugar
- 2   eggs, room temperature
- 1   tsp. vanilla
- 1   cup apple butter
- 3   medium apples, cored and finely chopped (3 cups)
- 1   14-oz. can dulce de leche
- ¼   cup milk
- 1   recipe Caramel Whipped Cream

1. Preheat oven to 350°F. Grease a 13×9-inch baking pan.

2. In a medium bowl whisk together first four ingredients (through salt).

3. In a large bowl beat butter with a mixer on medium 30 seconds. Gradually add sugar, ¼ cup at a time, beating on medium until combined. Scrape bowl; beat 2 minutes. Add eggs, one at a time, beating after each. Beat in vanilla. Alternately, add the flour mixture and apple butter, beating on low after each addition until well combined. Fold in apples. Spread batter into prepared pan.

4. Bake 30 to 35 minutes or until golden and a toothpick inserted near center comes out clean. Cool in pan on a wire rack 5 minutes. Meanwhile, in a medium bowl whisk together the dulce de leche and milk until smooth.

5. Using the handle of a wooden spoon, poke holes through cake about 1 inch apart. Spread dulce de leche mixture over cake. Cool completely. Spread with Caramel Whipped Cream. Makes 16 servings.

Caramel Whipped Cream In a large chilled bowl beat 1 cup heavy cream, 2 tablespoons caramel-flavor ice cream topping, and 1 teaspoon vanilla with a mixer on medium until stiff peaks form.

PER SERVING *426 cal., 16 g fat (10 g sat. fat), 68 mg chol., 297 mg sodium, 66 g carb., 2 g fiber, 48 g sugars, 5 g pro.*

PEAR AND CRANBERRY CROSTATA

PEAR AND CRANBERRY CROSTATA

PREP 20 minutes
CHILL 30 minutes
BAKE 45 minutes at 400°F

- 1   cup all-purpose flour
- 6   Tbsp. sugar
- ⅛   tsp. salt
- ¼   cup reduced-fat cream cheese (neufchâtel), chilled
- 2   Tbsp. vegetable shortening, chilled
- ⅓   cup sweetened dried cranberries
- 3   Tbsp. apple or orange juice
- 3   Bartlett pears (about 1½ lb.)
- 1   Tbsp. cornstarch
- ½   tsp. ground cinnamon
- 1   egg yolk, lightly beaten

1. In a bowl whisk flour, 3 tablespoons sugar, and the salt. With a pastry blender, cut in cream cheese and shortening until coarse crumbs form. Sprinkle with 3 tablespoons cold water, 1 tablespoon at a time, just until dough holds together. Shape into a 6-inch disk. Wrap well; refrigerate 30 minutes.

2. In a small microwave-safe bowl combine cranberries and juice. Microwave 30 seconds; set aside.

3. Preheat oven to 400°F. Peel and core pears; halve and cut into thin slices. In a large bowl combine pears, 2 tablespoons sugar, the cornstarch, and cinnamon. Stir in cranberries and any liquid.

4. On a lightly floured surface, with floured rolling pin, roll pastry to a 13-inch circle. Roll pastry onto pin; unroll onto large ungreased baking sheet. Mound pear filling in center, leaving a 2½-inch border. Fold border partway over filling (crostata should measure 8 inches across). Brush edge with egg yolk; sprinkle with remaining 1 tablespoon sugar.

5. Bake 40 to 45 minutes or until pears are tender. Makes 8 servings.

*Tip If dough becomes too soft to work with, refrigerate on baking sheet before filling.

PER SERVING *204 cal., 5 g fat (2 g sat. fat), 28 mg chol., 68 mg sodium, 40 g carb., 3 g fiber, 22 g sugars, 3 g pro.*

TRES LECHES BREAD PUDDING

BERRY COBBLER WITH BROWN SUGAR-PECAN BISCUITS

PREP 30 minutes
BAKE 35 minutes at 375°F
COOL 20 minutes

1   lemon
8   cups fresh blackberries and/or blueberries
¾   cup granulated sugar
2   Tbsp. cornstarch
¼   tsp. salt
1   tsp. grated fresh ginger
1   recipe Brown Sugar-Pecan Biscuits
1   recipe Sweetened Whipped Cream

1. Preheat oven to 375°F. Remove 2 teaspoons zest and squeeze 3 tablespoons juice from lemon. Place berries in a 3-quart rectangular baking dish. Sprinkle with the lemon juice. In a small bowl combine sugar, cornstarch, and salt. Stir in lemon zest and ginger. Sprinkle sugar mixture over berries; gently stir into berries.
2. Arrange Brown Sugar-Pecan Biscuits on berry mixture. Bake 25 minutes. Cover loosely with foil; bake 10 to 20 minutes more or until filling is bubbly around edges. Remove foil. Cool on a wire rack at least 20 minutes before serving. Serve with Sweetened Whipped Cream. Makes 8 servings.
Brown Sugar-Pecan Biscuits Place ½ cup toasted pecans in a food processor. Pulse until coarsely chopped. Add 1¾ cups all-purpose flour, ½ cup packed brown sugar, 2½ teaspoons baking powder, ½ teaspoon baking soda, and ½ teaspoon salt. Pulse until combined. Add ¼ cup cold butter, cut up. Pulse until pieces are pea size. Transfer flour mixture to a large bowl. Add ⅔ cup buttermilk. Using a fork, stir just until moistened. Turn dough out onto a lightly floured surface. Knead dough by folding and gently pressing just until dough holds together. Pat or lightly roll dough into a ½-inch-thick rectangle or circle. Cut dough into eight 2½-inch squares or rounds, rerolling scraps as necessary. Brush tops of biscuits with additional buttermilk; sprinkle with additional granulated sugar.

TRES LECHES BREAD PUDDING

PREP 30 minutes
BAKE 40 minutes at 350°F
COOL 10 minutes

4   cups 1-inch cubes dried* bolillo rolls or French baguette (about 6 oz.)
½   cup golden raisins or snipped dried prunes or apricots
¼   cup chopped roasted, salted pistachio nuts; toasted almonds; or walnuts (optional)
1   14-oz. can sweetened condensed milk
⅔   cup plus 2 to 3 Tbsp. milk
1   5-oz. can evaporated milk
2   eggs, lightly beaten
¼   cup butter, melted
¼   cup granulated sugar or packed brown sugar
1   tsp. ground cinnamon
1   tsp. vanilla
2   oz. Mexican or semisweet chocolate, chopped

1. Preheat oven to 350°F. Grease a 2-quart square baking dish. Place bread cubes, raisins, and, if desired, nuts in the dish. In a medium bowl whisk together ⅔ cup of the sweetened condensed milk, ⅔ cup milk, and the next six ingredients (through vanilla). Pour over bread mixture in dish. Use a spatula to press bread into the milk mixture.
2. Bake, uncovered, 40 minutes or until puffed and a knife inserted near center comes out clean. Cool 10 minutes.
3. Meanwhile, in a small saucepan melt chocolate over low. Stir in remaining sweetened condensed milk and 2 to 3 tablespoons milk to reach drizzling consistency. Drizzle chocolate over bread pudding. Makes 8 servings.
*Tip To dry bread, spread bread cubes in a 15×10-inch baking pan. Cover loosely and let stand overnight, or bake in a 300°F oven 10 to 15 minutes, stirring every 5 minutes. Bread will continue to dry as it cools.
PER SERVING *440 cal., 17 g fat (9 g sat. fat), 86 mg chol., 280 mg sodium, 63 g carb., 2 g fiber, 48 g sugars, 11 g pro.*

BERRY COBBLER WITH BROWN SUGAR-PECAN BISCUITS

Sweetened Whipped Cream In a chilled medium bowl beat 1 cup whipping cream, 2 tablespoons sugar, and ½ teaspoon vanilla with a mixer on medium until soft peaks form (tips curl).
PER SERVING 491 cal., 18 g fat (8 g sat. fat), 39 mg chol., 495 mg sodium, 81 g carb., 7 g fiber, 49 g sugars, 6 g pro.

PEAR, APPLE, AND CRANBERRY COBBLER

PREP 35 minutes
BAKE 50 minutes at 375°F
COOL 30 minutes

- 4 medium ripe pears, peeled, cored, and chopped
- 3 medium cooking apples, peeled, cored, and chopped
- 2 cups cranberries
- 1 cup sugar
- 3 Tbsp. all-purpose flour
- 2 tsp. orange zest
- 1 tsp. lemon juice
- ⅛ tsp. salt
- ¾ cup all-purpose flour
- ¼ cup cornmeal
- 2 Tbsp. sugar
- 1½ tsp. baking powder
- ¼ cup butter, cut up
- ⅓ cup milk, half-and-half, or light cream
- 1 egg, lightly beaten
  Vanilla ice cream or whipped cream (optional)

1. Preheat oven to 375°F. In a large bowl combine pears, apples, cranberries, 1 cup sugar, 3 tablespoons flour, the orange zest, lemon juice, and salt. Toss lightly just until combined. Spoon into a 2-quart casserole dish. Bake, uncovered, 25 minutes.

2. Meanwhile, in a medium bowl combine ¾ cup flour, the cornmeal, 2 tablespoons sugar, and the baking powder. Using a pastry blender, cut butter into flour mixture until butter is pea size. Combine milk and egg. Add to flour mixture all at once, stirring just until combined. Spoon eight mounds on fruit mixture.

3. Bake 25 minutes or until a toothpick inserted near center of topping comes out clean. Cool 30 minutes. Serve warm with ice cream, if desired. Makes 8 servings.
PER SERVING 330 cal., 7 g fat (4 g sat. fat), 43 mg chol., 139 mg sodium, 66 g carb., 6 g fiber, 44 g sugars, 4 g pro.

PEAR, APPLE, AND CRANBERRY COBBLER

CHERRY-
PISTACHIO
CRISP

CHERRY-PISTACHIO CRISP

PREP 45 minutes
BAKE 40 minutes at 375°F
COOL 30 minutes

- 2 lb. fresh or frozen* dark sweet cherries, stemmed and pitted (about 6 cups)
- 3 Tbsp. granulated sugar
- ½ tsp. lemon zest
- 1 Tbsp. lemon juice
- 2 tsp. cornstarch
- ¾ cup sliced almonds
- ½ cup whole wheat pastry flour
- ½ cup regular rolled oats
- ½ cup salted roasted pistachio nuts
- 3 Tbsp. packed brown sugar
- 2 tsp. baking powder
- ½ tsp. baking soda
- ¼ tsp. salt
- ¼ tsp. ground cinnamon
- 6 Tbsp. cold butter, cut into ½-inch pieces
- ¼ cup buttermilk

1. Preheat oven to 375°F. Grease a 2-quart rectangular baking dish; set aside.
2. For filling, in a large bowl toss together cherries, granulated sugar, lemon zest, lemon juice, and cornstarch. Spoon into prepared baking dish.
3. For topping, place almonds in a food processor. Cover and process until finely ground. Add pastry flour, oats, pistachio nuts, brown sugar, baking powder, baking soda, salt, and cinnamon. Pulse until combined. Add butter; pulse until mixture resembles coarse cornmeal. With machine running, add buttermilk.
4. Crumble topping over filling in baking dish. Bake 40 minutes or until topping is browned and filling is bubbly. Cool in pan on a wire rack 30 minutes; serve warm. Makes 10 servings.

*Tip To use frozen cherries, spread 6 cups cherries in a shallow baking pan; thaw at room temperature 30 to 40 minutes or until cherries soften yet maintain their shape. Drain, discarding juices.

PER SERVING *260 cal., 14 g fat (5 g sat. fat), 19 mg chol., 290 mg sodium, 33 g carb., 4 g fiber, 21 g sugars, 5 g pro.*

STONE FRUIT-COCONUT CRISP

STONE FRUIT-COCONUT CRISP

PREP 40 minutes
BAKE 25 minutes at 375°F

- 4 cups fresh or frozen pitted Royal Ann or dark sweet cherries
- 1 to 2 oranges
- ½ cup granulated sugar
- 3 Tbsp. cornstarch
- 6 cups sliced stone fruit, such as nectarines, plums, and/or peeled peaches
- ¾ cup rolled oats
- ½ cup packed brown sugar
- ⅓ cup all-purpose flour
- ⅓ cup butter, cut up
- 1 cup flaked coconut
  Coconut ice cream or sorbet (optional)

1. If using frozen cherries, let stand at room temperature 30 minutes (do not drain). Preheat oven to 375°F. Remove 1 tablespoon zest and squeeze ½ cup juice from oranges. In a 4- to 6-quart Dutch oven stir together granulated sugar and cornstarch. Stir in cherries, stone fruit, and orange juice. Cook and stir over medium until thickened and bubbly. Transfer to a 13×9-inch baking dish.
2. For topping, in a bowl stir together oats, brown sugar, flour, and orange zest. Cut in butter until mixture resembles coarse crumbs. Stir in coconut. Sprinkle topping over fruit mixture.
3. Bake 25 minutes or until stone fruit is tender and topping is golden. Serve warm. If desired, serve with ice cream. Makes 8 servings.

PER SERVING *420 cal., 13 g fat (9 g sat. fat), 20 mg chol., 103 mg sodium, 74 g carb., 6 g fiber, 53 g sugars, 5 g pro.*

BRIOCHE BREAD PUDDING MUFFINS WITH MAPLE CARAMEL

PREP 10 minutes
BAKE 20 minutes at 300°F plus 30 minutes at 350°F
STAND 30 minutes
COOL 10 minutes

8   oz. brioche, cut into ¾-inch cubes (about 6 cups)
     Butter, softened
2   cups buttermilk
5   Tbsp. unsalted butter, melted
⅓   cup plus 2 Tbsp. packed light brown sugar
2   eggs
2¼   tsp. vanilla
¾   tsp. kosher salt
¼   cup pure maple syrup
2   Tbsp. heavy cream

1. Preheat oven to 300°F. Spread bread cubes evenly in a shallow baking pan. Bake 20 minutes or until crisp, stirring once; cool. Increase oven temperature to 350°F.
2. Butter six 3- to 3½-inch muffin cups or twelve 2½-inch muffin cups. Fill each cup with toasted bread.
3. In a large bowl whisk together buttermilk, melted butter, ⅓ cup brown sugar, the eggs, 2 teaspoons vanilla, and ¼ teaspoon kosher salt. Slowly pour mixture over bread in each cup. Cover; let stand 30 minutes or chill up to 4 hours.
4. Meanwhile, for maple caramel, in a small saucepan combine maple syrup and remaining 2 tablespoons brown sugar. Bring to boiling; reduce heat. Boil gently 2 minutes, stirring occasionally. Remove from heat; carefully add cream and the remaining ¼ teaspoon vanilla and ½ teaspoon salt. Return to heat; boil gently 1 minute, stirring constantly. Remove from heat. Caramel will thicken as it cools.
5. Bake muffins 30 to 35 minutes or until puffed, golden brown, and set.

Cool 10 minutes. Remove muffins from cups. Serve warm drizzled with Maple Caramel. Makes 6 servings.
PER SERVING *432 cal., 26 g fat (15 g sat. fat), 161 mg chol., 474 mg sodium, 44 g carb., 0 g fiber, 31 g sugars, 8 g pro.*

PUMPKIN-CHOCOLATE CREAM CHEESE SLAB PIE

PREP 30 minutes
BAKE 25 minutes at 350°F

     Nonstick cooking spray
6   oz. bittersweet chocolate, chopped
⅓   cup heavy cream
1   Tbsp. butter
1   8-oz. pkg. cream cheese, softened
½   cup sugar
1   tsp. vanilla
1   egg
2   cups all-purpose flour
1½   cups sugar
2   tsp. baking powder
2   tsp. ground cinnamon
1   tsp. baking soda
½   tsp. salt
1   15-oz. can pumpkin
4   eggs
1   cup vegetable oil

1. Preheat oven to 350°F. Line a 15×10-inch baking pan with foil; coat foil with nonstick cooking spray.
2. In a small saucepan heat chocolate, cream, and butter over low heat, stirring just until melted. Set aside to cool and thicken slightly.
3. In a medium bowl beat cream cheese until smooth. Add ½ sugar and the vanilla; beat until combined. Add 1 egg; beat on low just until combined.
4. In a large bowl whisk together flour, 1½ cups sugar, the baking powder, cinnamon, baking soda, and salt. In a medium bowl whisk together pumpkin, 4 eggs, and oil. Add to flour mixture. Whisk until smooth. Pour batter into prepared pan.
5. Alternately spoon chocolate and cream cheese mixtures over pumpkin mixture in pan. Bake 25 to 30 minutes or until set. Remove and cool completely on a wire rack.
6. Use foil to lift slab pie from pan. Cut into bars. Chill to store. Makes 36 servings.
PER SERVING *193 cal., 12 g fat (4 g sat. fat), 36 mg chol., 128 mg sodium, 21 g carb., 1 g fiber, 14 g sugars, 2 g pro.*

BRIOCHE BREAD PUDDING MUFFINS WITH MAPLE CARAMEL

APPLE-ALMOND
BETTY

APPLE-ALMOND BETTY

PREP 20 minutes
COOK 10 minutes
BAKE 40 minutes at 375°F

1	7-oz. pkg. amaretti cookies
6	Tbsp. cold unsalted butter
¾	tsp. kosher salt
3	lb. crisp, tart apples, such as Granny Smith, peeled, cored, and halved
½	cup packed light brown sugar
2	Tbsp. cornstarch
½	tsp. ground cinnamon
1	Tbsp. bourbon (optional)
1	lemon, zested
	Vanilla ice cream or heavy cream (optional)

1. Preheat oven to 375°F. Line a rimmed baking sheet with parchment paper or foil. Place a 9-inch pie plate or similar ovenproof dish on baking sheet.
2. Place cookies in a food processor and pulse to fine crumbs. Add 4 tablespoons butter and ¼ teaspoon salt. Pulse to moist crumbs; set aside.
3. Slice apples about ⅛ inch thick. In an extra-large skillet melt the remaining 2 tablespoons butter over medium. Add apples; toss to coat. Cook, covered, until apples are softened, 7 to 9 minutes, stirring occasionally.
4. Meanwhile, in a small bowl stir together brown sugar, cornstarch, cinnamon, and the remaining ½ teaspoon salt. Add sugar mixture to apples and cook until juices thicken to a syrup, 1 to 2 minutes. Stir in bourbon, if using, and lemon zest.

5. Scatter ½ cup of the crumb mixture across bottom of pie plate. Spoon in one-third of the apples and their syrup. Repeat twice, using all the apples. Top with remaining crumbs.
6. Bake, uncovered, until golden brown and juices bubble thickly, 40 minutes. Serve warm with ice cream or drizzle with cream. If desired, sprinkle with additional cinnamon. Makes 6 servings.
Tip If desired, assemble the recipe in six individual-size ovenproof ramekins. Reduce baking time to about 20 minutes.
PER SERVING *447 cal., 16 g fat (7 g sat. fat), 31 mg chol., 163 mg sodium, 73 g carb., 7 g fiber, 61 g sugars, 4 g pro.*

PEPPERMINT-FUDGE PIE

PREP 50 minutes
BAKE 7 minutes at 375°F
FREEZE 8 hours

1   recipe Chocolate Crumb Crust
1¾ cup sugar
1   5-oz. can evaporated milk
2   Tbsp. butter
2   oz. unsweetened chocolate, cut up
1   tsp. vanilla
2   pints peppermint ice cream
    Sweetened Whipped Cream (recipe, opposite)
    Small candy canes

1. Prepare Chocolate Crumb Crust. For fudge sauce, in a small saucepan combine 1 cup sugar, the evaporated milk, butter, and chocolate. Cook and stir over medium until bubbly; reduce heat. Boil gently 4 to 5 minutes or until mixture is thickened and reduced to 1½ cups, stirring occasionally. Remove from heat; stir in vanilla. If necessary, beat until smooth with a wire whisk or rotary beater. Cool completely.
2. In a chilled bowl stir 1 pint peppermint ice cream until softened. Spread on cooled Chocolate Crumb Crust. Place cooled fudge sauce in a pastry bag fitted with a round tip, about ¼ inch in diameter.* Pipe half the cooled fudge sauce over ice cream. Freeze 2 hours or until nearly firm. Repeat layers with remaining ice cream and fudge sauce. Return to freezer for 6 hours or until firm.
3. Serve with Sweetened Whipped Cream and a candy cane, if desired. Makes 12 servings.

*Tip In place of a pastry bag, spoon small spoonfuls of fudge sauce over ice cream layer; spread evenly.

Make Ahead Prepare as directed. Place pie in a freezer bag. Freeze up to 4 months.
Chocolate Crumb Crust Preheat oven to 375°F. Lightly coat an 8-inch springform pan with nonstick cooking spray; set aside. In a medium bowl combine 1 cup finely crushed vanilla wafers (about 30 cookies), ⅓ cup powdered sugar, and 3 tablespoons unsweetened cocoa powder. Stir in 3 tablespoons melted butter. Press crumb mixture firmly into bottom of prepared pan. Bake 7 to 8 minutes or until crust is firm. Cool in pan on a wire rack.
PER SERVING *357 cal., 12 fat (7 g sat. fat), 19 mg chol., 122 mg sodium, 60 g carb., 1 g fiber, 49 g sugars, 3 g pro.*

PEPPERMINT-FUDGE PIE

GÂTEAU AU CHOCOLATE

PREP 20 minutes
BAKE 35 minutes at 350°F
COOL 20 minutes

- 2 tsp. unsalted butter, softened
- 1 Tbsp. unsweetened cocoa powder
- 8 oz. good-quality bittersweet (about 60%) chocolate, such as Ghirardelli
- 12 Tbsp. unsalted butter, cut into chunks
- 3 large eggs
- 1 cup sugar
- ¾ tsp. kosher salt
- ½ cup sifted all-purpose flour
- 1 recipe Sweetened Whipped Cream

1. Preheat oven to 350°F. Grease an 8-inch springform pan with softened butter. Dust with cocoa powder; tap out excess.
2. Break bittersweet chocolate into a medium microwave-safe bowl. Add butter chunks. Microwave 1 minute. Stir. Microwave 30 seconds; stir until smooth.
3. In a large bowl beat eggs with a mixer on high, gradually adding sugar and salt, until pale, thick, and tripled in volume, about 3 minutes.
4. Pour chocolate mixture into egg mixture; beat on low to combine. Sprinkle in flour; beat on low just until combined. Pour batter in prepared pan.

5. Bake 35 minutes or until puffed, surface is dry, and a toothpick inserted in center comes out clean. Cool in pan on wire rack 20 minutes; remove sides of pan. Serve warm or at room temperature with Sweetened Whipped Cream. Makes 12 servings.
Sweetened Whipped Cream In a chilled medium bowl beat 1 cup whipping cream, 2 tablespoons sugar, and ½ teaspoon vanilla with a mixer on medium until soft peaks form (tips curl).
PER SERVING *378 cal., 28 g fat (17 g sat. fat), 102 mg chol., 101 mg sodium, 33 g carb., 2 g fiber, 26 g sugars, 4 g pro.*

GÂTEAU AU CHOCOLATE

MEXICAN CHOCOLATE
POTS DE CRÈME

CHERRY-PECAN CRÈME BRÛLÉE

Photo, page 77
PREP 20 minutes
BAKE 35 minutes at 325°F
CHILL 1 hour
STAND 20 minutes

3 cups whipping cream
¾ cup dried tart cherries (about 3 oz.)
¾ cup chopped pecans
8 egg yolks, lightly beaten
¼ cup sugar
1 tsp. vanilla
⅓ cup sugar

1. Preheat oven to 325°F. In a medium-size heavy saucepan heat cream over medium-low just until bubbly, stirring occasionally. Meanwhile, divide cherries and pecans among eight 6-ounce custard cups or five 8-ounce individual baking dishes.
2. In a large bowl combine egg yolks, ¼ cup sugar, and the vanilla. Gradually add heated whipping cream. Place custard cups or baking dishes in a large shallow baking pan. Pour egg yolk mixture into dishes. Set pan on oven rack. Pour enough hot water into pan to reach about halfway up sides of dishes.
3. Bake 35 to 40 minutes or until a knife inserted near centers comes out clean. Remove pan from oven. Carefully lift dishes from water bath. Cool on wire racks. Cover and chill at least 1 hour.
4. Before serving, let custards stand at room temperature 20 minutes. Meanwhile, place ⅓ cup sugar in a small heavy saucepan. Place over medium-high heat until sugar begins to melt, shaking saucepan occasionally to heat sugar evenly. Don't stir. After sugar starts to melt, reduce heat to low and cook 5 minutes more or until all the sugar is melted and golden, stirring as needed with a wooden spoon.
5. Quickly drizzle caramelized sugar over custards. If sugar starts to harden in the saucepan, return to heat, stirring until melted. Serve immediately. Makes 8 regular or 5 large servings.
PER REGULAR SERVING *539 cal., 44 g fat (23 g sat. fat), 286 mg chol., 35 mg sodium, 31 g carb., 1 g fiber, 28 g sugars, 6 g pro.*

MEXICAN CHOCOLATE POTS DE CRÈME

PREP 25 minutes
BAKE 25 minutes at 325°F
COOL 1 hour

2 cups whipping cream
3 oz. milk chocolate, coarsely chopped
¼ tsp. ground cinnamon
5 egg yolks, lightly beaten
¼ cup sugar
1 tsp. vanilla
¼ tsp. salt
⅛ tsp. almond extract
Ground cinnamon (optional)

1. Preheat oven to 325°F. In a medium-size heavy saucepan heat and stir ⅓ cup whipping cream and the chocolate over low until chocolate is melted. Remove from heat. Gradually stir in remaining 1⅔ cups whipping cream and ¼ teaspoon cinnamon.

2. In a large bowl combine egg yolks, sugar, vanilla, salt, and almond extract. Gradually stir in chocolate mixture.
3. Place eight 4-ounce ramekins in a 13×9-inch baking pan or shallow roasting pan. Divide chocolate mixture among ramekins. Place baking pan on oven rack. Pour enough boiling water into baking pan to reach halfway up sides of ramekins.
4. Bake 25 minutes or until centers appear set when gently shaken. Remove ramekins from water. Cool on a wire rack 1 hour to serve warm, or cover and chill up to 6 hours. If chilled, let stand at room temperature 30 minutes before serving. If desired, sprinkle with additional cinnamon. Makes 8 servings.
PER SERVING *324 cal., 28 g fat (17 g sat. fat), 216 mg chol., 109 mg sodium, 15 g carb., 0 g fiber, 12 g sugars, 4 g pro.*

CITRUS-PUMPKIN FLANS

PREP 15 minutes
BAKE 40 minutes at 325°F
CHILL 4 hours

⅔ cup sugar
3 eggs, beaten
¾ cup canned pumpkin
1 5-oz. can (⅔ cup) evaporated milk
¼ cup sugar
1 tsp. pumpkin pie spice
1 tsp. orange zest
1 tsp. vanilla
Pomegranate seeds (optional)

1. Preheat oven to 325°F. To caramelize sugar, in a medium-size heavy skillet melt ⅔ cup sugar over medium-high. Do not stir; shake skillet occasionally.

When sugar starts to melt, reduce heat to low. Cook, stirring frequently with a wooden spoon, until sugar is golden brown.
2. Remove skillet from heat and immediately pour caramelized sugar into four ungreased 6-ounce custard cups. Holding cups with pot holders, quickly tilt to evenly coat bottoms of cups.
3. Place cups in a 2-quart square baking pan. In a bowl stir together eggs, pumpkin, milk, ¼ cup sugar, the pumpkin pie spice, orange zest, and vanilla. Pour pumpkin mixture over caramelized sugar in cups. Place pan on oven rack. Pour boiling water into baking pan around cups to a depth of 1 inch.

4. Bake 40 to 45 minutes or until a knife inserted near centers comes out clean. Remove cups from water. Cool slightly on a wire rack. Cover and chill 4 to 24 hours
5. To serve, loosen edges of flans with a knife, slipping knife point down the sides to let in air. Invert a dessert plate over each flan; turn over custard cup and plate together. Scrape the caramelized sugar that remains in cup onto the flan. If desired, top with pomegranate seeds. Makes 4 servings.
PER SERVING *293 cal., 4 g fat (2 g sat. fat), 139 mg chol., 92 mg sodium, 57 g carb., 1 g fiber, 51 g sugars, 8 g pro.*

The Cookie Collection

Say Christmas sweetly with batches of homemade cookies, bars, and no-bake treats—simple or decorated to the hilt.

GINGERBREAD
CUTOUTS,
PAGE 107

CHERRY-WHITE CHOCOLATE
CHIP COOKIES, PAGE 96

CHERRY-WHITE CHOCOLATE CHIP COOKIES

Photo, page 95
PREP 25 minutes
BAKE 6 minutes per batch at 375°F

- ½ cup shortening
- ½ cup butter, softened
- 1½ cups granulated sugar
- 1 tsp. baking soda
- 1 tsp. kosher salt
- 2 eggs
- 2 Tbsp. maraschino cherry juice
  Pink food coloring (optional)
- 2¾ cups all-purpose flour
- 4 oz. white baking chocolate, chopped
- ½ cup chopped stemmed maraschino cherries, patted dry
- 4 oz. white baking chocolate with cocoa, chopped (optional)
- 1 Tbsp. shortening (optional)

1. Preheat oven to 375°F. In a large bowl beat ½ cup shortening and the butter with a mixer on medium 30 seconds. Add sugar, baking soda, and salt. Beat on medium 2 minutes, scraping bowl as needed. Beat in eggs, cherry juice, and food coloring (if using) until combined. Beat in flour. Stir in 4 ounces white chocolate and the chopped cherries.
2. Drop dough by rounded teaspoons 2 inches apart onto ungreased cookie sheets. Bake 6 to 8 minutes or just until starting to turn brown. Cool on cookie sheets 2 minutes. Remove; cool on wire racks.
3. If desired, in a bowl microwave 4 ounces white chocolate with cocoa and 1 tablespoon shortening in 30-second intervals until melted, stirring until smooth. Dip cookies partway into melted chocolate, let excess drip off, and place on wire racks over waxed paper. Let set. Makes 48 servings.
PER SERVING 108 cal., 5 g fat (2 g sat. fat), 13 mg chol., 70 mg sodium, 15 g carb., 0 g fiber, 9 g sugars, 1 g pro.

CRISPY TAHINI CHOCOLATE CHIPPERS

PREP 20 minutes
BAKE 10 minutes per batch at 350°F
STAND 30 minutes

- ½ cup butter, softened
- ½ cup tahini (sesame seed paste)
- 1 cup granulated sugar
- ⅔ cup packed brown sugar
- 1 tsp. baking soda
- ½ tsp. salt
- 2 eggs
- 1 tsp. vanilla
- 2 cups all-purpose flour
- 1 10- to 12-oz. pkg. dark chocolate chips
- 1 recipe Tahini Icing
  Sesame seeds

1. Preheat oven to 350°F. Line cookie sheets with parchment paper. In a large bowl beat butter and tahini with a mixer on medium to high until well blended. Add sugars, baking soda, and salt. Beat on medium 2 minutes, scraping bowl as needed. Beat in eggs and vanilla until combined. Beat in as much of the flour as you can with the mixer. Stir in any remaining flour and chocolate chips.
2. Drop dough by rounded tablespoons 2 inches apart onto prepared cookie sheets. Bake 10 to 12 minutes or until lightly browned. Cool on cookie sheets 5 minutes. Remove; cool on wire racks.
3. Drizzle Tahini Icing on cooled cookies and sprinkle with sesame seeds. Let stand 30 minutes or until set. Makes 48 servings.
Tahini Icing In a small bowl whisk together 2 tablespoons tahini (sesame seed paste), 1 cup powdered sugar, and 2 to 3 tablespoons milk to reach drizzling consistency.
PER SERVING 124 cal., 6 g fat (3 g sat. fat), 13 mg chol., 3 mg sodium, 18 g carb., 1 g fiber, 13 g sugars, 2 g pro.

CRISPY TAHINI CHOCOLATE CHIPPERS

BROWNED BUTTER-TOFFEE CHOCOLATE CHIP COOKIES

PREP 25 minutes
BAKE 8 minutes per batch at 350°F

1	cup butter
1	cup packed brown sugar
½	cup granulated sugar
2	tsp. baking powder
½	tsp. salt
2	eggs
1	tsp. vanilla
1¼	cups all-purpose flour
3	cups regular or quick-cooking rolled oats*
2	1.4-oz. chocolate-covered toffee candy bars (½ cup) or ½ cup toffee almond bits
1	cup milk chocolate chips
½	cup chopped pecans (optional)

1. Preheat oven to 350°F. In a large skillet heat butter over medium 5 minutes or until butter turns golden brown. Immediately remove from heat. Pour into a large bowl; cool 5 minutes.
2. Add sugars, baking powder, and salt to butter; beat with a mixer on medium to high 30 seconds. Beat in eggs and vanilla. Beat in flour. Stir in oats, chopped candy bars, milk chocolate chips, and pecans (if using).
3. Drop dough by rounded tablespoons 2 inches apart onto ungreased cookie sheets. Bake 8 to 10 minutes or until light brown and centers appear set. Cool on cookie sheets 2 minutes. Remove; cool on wire racks. Makes 42 servings.
*Tip If using quick-cooking oats, add 1 tablespoon milk to dough with the eggs.
PER SERVING *144 cal., 7 g fat (4 g sat. fat), 23 mg chol., 101 mg sodium, 19 g carb., 1 g fiber, 12 g sugars, 2 g pro.*

BROWNED BUTTER-TOFFEE CHOCOLATE CHIP COOKIES

COOKIES AND CREAM ICEBOX COOKIES

PREP 30 minutes
CHILL 1 hour
BAKE 7 minutes per batch at 375°F

⅔	cup butter, softened
¾	cup granulated sugar
1	tsp. baking powder
¼	tsp. salt
1	egg
1	tsp. vanilla
2	cups all-purpose flour
1	cup crushed chocolate sandwich cookies with white filling (about 10 cookies)

1. In a large bowl beat butter with a mixer on medium to high 30 seconds. Add sugar, baking powder, and salt. Beat until combined, scraping bowl as needed. Beat in egg and vanilla. Beat in as much of the flour as you can with the mixer. Stir in any remaining flour. Stir in ¾ cup crushed cookies. If necessary, cover and chill dough until easy to handle.
2. Shape dough into a 2-inch-diameter log. Coat log with remaining ¼ cup crushed cookies. Wrap in plastic wrap or waxed paper; chill until firm enough to slice (1 to 2 hours in refrigerator or 30 minutes in freezer).
3. Preheat oven to 375°F. Use a serrated knife to cut log into ¼-inch slices; place slices 2 inches apart on an ungreased cookie sheet.
4. Bake 7 to 9 minutes or until bottoms are lightly browned. Cool on cookie sheet 2 minutes. Remove; cool on wire rack. Makes 24 servings.
PER SERVING *133 cal., 6 g fat (4 g sat. fat), 21 mg chol., 108 mg sodium, 18 g carb., 0 g fiber, 8 g sugars, 2 g pro.*

**COOKIES AND
CREAM ICEBOX
COOKIES**

ICED WALNUT
SHORTBREAD
ROUNDS

ICED WALNUT
SHORTBREAD ROUNDS

PREP 30 minutes
BAKE 18 minutes at 325°F

1¼ cups all-purpose flour
½ cup toasted walnuts, ground (tip, page 24)
¼ cup granulated sugar
⅛ tsp. salt
½ cup butter
2 oz. cream cheese, softened
2 Tbsp. butter, softened
1 cup powdered sugar
Milk
Coarse sugar or granulated sugar (optional)

1. Preheat oven to 325°F. In a large bowl stir together flour, ground walnuts, ¼ cup granulated sugar, and the salt. Using a pastry blender, cut in ½ cup butter until mixture resembles fine crumbs and starts to cling. Form mixture into a ball and knead until smooth.
2. On a lightly floured surface, roll dough to ¼-inch thickness. Using a 2-inch scalloped-edge round cookie cutter, cut out dough. Place cutouts on a large ungreased cookie sheet.
3. Bake 18 to 22 minutes or just until edges start to brown. Remove; cool on a wire rack.
4. For icing, in a medium bowl beat cream cheese and 2 tablespoons

butter with a mixer on medium until smooth. Gradually add powdered sugar, beating until combined. Beat in enough milk for icing to reach drizzling consistency. Drizzle icing over cookies. If desired, sprinkle with coarse sugar. Makes 14 servings.
PER SERVING *196 cal., 12 g fat (6 g sat. fat), 26 mg chol., 105 mg sodium, 22 g carb., 0 g fiber, 13 g sugars, 2 g pro.*

PINK GRAPEFRUIT SANDIES

PINK GRAPEFRUIT SANDIES

PREP 30 minutes
CHILL 30 minutes
BAKE 15 minutes per batch at 325°F

1   cup butter, softened
2½ cups powdered sugar
1   Tbsp. water
1   tsp. vanilla
2   cups all-purpose flour
1½ cups slivered almonds, toasted and finely chopped (tip, page 24)
1   tsp. grapefruit zest
3   to 4 Tbsp. pink grapefruit juice
     Red or pink food coloring (optional)
     Coarse decorating sugar or pink sprinkles

1. In a large bowl beat butter with a mixer on medium 30 seconds. Add ½ cup of the powdered sugar. Beat until combined, scraping bowl as needed. Beat in water and vanilla until combined. Beat in as much of the flour as you can with the mixer. Stir in any remaining flour. Stir in almonds and grapefruit zest. Cover and chill 30 to 60 minutes or until firm enough to shape.

2. Preheat oven to 325°F. Shape dough into 1-inch balls. Place balls 1 inch apart on ungreased cookie sheets. Bake 15 minutes or until bottoms are light brown. Remove; cool on wire racks.

3. In a medium bowl stir together the remaining 2 cups powdered sugar and enough grapefruit juice to make drizzling consistency. If desired, tint lightly with food coloring. Dip balls in icing, allowing excess to drip back into bowl. Place on waxed paper. Top with coarse sugar before icing sets. Let stand until set. Makes 46 servings.

PER SERVING *104 cal., 6 g fat (3 g sat. fat), 11 mg chol., 32 mg sodium, 12 g carb., 1 g fiber, 7 g sugars, 1 g pro.*

TRIPLE-GINGER COOKIES

PREP 45 minutes
CHILL 1 hour
BAKE 10 minutes per batch at 350°F

2   cups all-purpose flour
1½   to 2 tsp. ground ginger
1   tsp. baking soda
1   tsp. ground cinnamon
¾   tsp. salt
½   to 1 tsp. ground cloves
½   to ¾ cup finely snipped
       crystallized ginger
½   cup shortening
¼   cup butter, softened
1   cup packed light brown sugar
1   egg
¼   cup dark molasses
¾   cup Ginger Sugar or granulated
       sugar

1. In a medium bowl stir together first six ingredients (through cloves). Stir in crystallized ginger.

2. In a large bowl beat shortening and butter with a mixer on medium 30 seconds. Add brown sugar and beat until combined, scraping bowl as needed. Beat in egg and molasses. Beat in flour mixture. Cover and chill 1 hour or until dough is easy to handle.

3. Preheat oven to 350°F. Lightly grease cookie sheets. Place Ginger Sugar in a small bowl. Shape dough into 1-inch balls. Roll balls in Ginger Sugar to coat. Place balls 1½ inches apart on prepared cookie sheets.

4. Bake 10 to 12 minutes or until edges are set. Cool on cookie sheets 1 minute. Remove; cool on wire racks. Makes 48 servings.

PER SERVING *88 cal., 3 g fat (1 g sat. fat), 6 mg chol., 76 mg sodium, 14 g carb., 0 g fiber, 10 g sugars, 1 g pro.*

Ginger Sugar In a small bowl stir together ¾ cup granulated sugar and ¼ cup coarsely chopped fresh ginger. Let stand 1 hour (sugar will clump slightly from moisture in ginger). Place mixture in a fine-mesh sieve set over a bowl; stir gently to separate sugar from ginger. Discard ginger.

TRIPLE-GINGER COOKIES

COOKIE BUTTER
SANDWICH COOKIES

COOKIE BUTTER SANDWICH COOKIES

PREP 30 minutes
CHILL 30 minutes

1   cup purchased cookie butter or DIY Cookie Butter*
48   rich round crackers or small graham cracker rectangles
6   oz. semisweet or white baking chocolate
2   tsp. shortening
2   Tbsp. finely chopped toasted pecans

1. Line a tray or rimmed baking sheet with parchment paper or waxed paper. Spread cookie butter over half of the cracker bottoms. Top with remaining crackers, bottom sides down.
2. In a small bowl combine chocolate and shortening. Microwave 1 minute or until nearly melted, stirring twice. Stir until smooth. Dip cracker sandwiches partway into chocolate mixture to coat, allowing excess to drip off. Place on prepared tray. Sprinkle with pecans. Chill until set.
3. Refrigerate in an airtight container up to 1 week or freeze up to 3 months. Makes 24 servings.
PER SERVING *134 cal., 8 g fat (3 g sat. fat), 0 mg chol., 59 mg sodium, 14 g carb., 1 g fiber, 8 g sugars, 1 g pro.*
*DIY Cookie Butter In a medium saucepan heat and stir ½ cup milk, 3 tablespoons coconut oil or canola oil, 1 tablespoon packed brown sugar, ½ teaspoon pumpkin pie spice, and ⅛ teaspoon salt over medium and whisk until milk is warm and brown sugar is dissolved. Remove from heat. Stir in one 8.8-ounce package Biscoff cookies or 9-ounce package gingersnaps, coarsely broken; let stand 15 minutes. Transfer to a food processor or blender; add ½ teaspoon vanilla. Cover and process or blend until smooth, stopping to scrape sides as needed. Makes 1½ cups.

CREAM PIE WHOOPIE PIES

PREP 30 minutes
BAKE 10 minutes per batch at 350°F

½ cup shortening
1 cup granulated sugar
1 tsp. baking soda
¼ tsp. salt
1 egg
1¼ cups buttermilk
3 tsp. vanilla
2½ cups all-purpose flour
½ cup butter, softened
1 7-oz. jar marshmallow creme
1½ cups powdered sugar
Assorted sprinkles (optional)

1. Preheat oven to 350°F. Line cookie sheets with parchment paper. For cookies, in a large bowl beat shortening with a mixer on medium 30 seconds. Add granulated sugar, baking soda, and salt; beat until combined. Beat in egg, buttermilk, and 1 teaspoon vanilla. Beat in flour until combined.

2. Using a large cookie scoop, drop dough into 20 mounds, 2 inches apart, on prepared cookie sheets. Bake 10 minutes or until edges are firm and bottoms start to brown. Remove; cool on wire racks.

3. For filling, in a medium bowl beat butter with a mixer on medium 30 seconds. Beat in marshmallow creme and remaining 2 teaspoons vanilla until fluffy. Beat in powdered sugar.

4. Spread filling on bottoms of half the cookies. Press bottoms of remaining cookies against filling. If desired, roll edges of filled cookies in sprinkles Wrap individually and chill up to 3 days. Makes 10 servings.

PER SERVING *526 cal., 21 g fat (9 g sat. fat), 45 mg chol., 314 mg sodium, 79 g carb., 1 g fiber, 49 g sugars, 5 g pro.*

Banana Cream Whoopie Pies
Combine ½ cup mashed banana with 1 tablespoon lemon juice. Prepare cookies as directed, except beat half of the banana mixture into the cookie batter with the buttermilk and reduce buttermilk to 1 cup. Prepare filling as directed, except beat the remaining banana mixture into filling with the marshmallow creme and increase powdered sugar to 2½ cups.

CREAM PIE WHOOPIE PIES

Chocolate Cream Whoopie Pies
Prepare cookies as directed, except reduce flour to 2¼ cups and stir together with ¼ cup unsweetened cocoa powder before adding to batter. Prepare filling as directed, except add 1 tablespoon unsweetened cocoa powder with the powdered sugar.

Coconut Cream Whoopie Pies
Prepare cookies as directed. Prepare filling as directed, except add ¼ cup coconut cream solids to the butter, beating until smooth. Roll edges of filled cookies in toasted coconut.

Lemon Cream Whoopie Pies Prepare cookies as directed. Prepare filling as directed, except stir 2 teaspoons lemon zest into filling. If desired, roll edges of filled cookies in sprinkles.

Strawberry Cream Whoopie Pies
Prepare cookies as directed, except add ⅛ teaspoon liquid red food coloring to batter with the buttermilk. Prepare filling as directed, except fold in 6 tablespoons finely crushed freeze-dried strawberries after preparing filling.

LEMON-CREAM
ICEBOX COOKIE
SANDWICHES

LEMON-CREAM ICEBOX COOKIE SANDWICHES

PREP 30 minutes
CHILL 2 hours
BAKE 8 minutes per batch at 375°F

½ cup butter-flavor shortening
½ cup butter, softened
1 cup granulated sugar
1 tsp. baking powder
¼ tsp. salt
1 egg
1 tsp. vanilla
2¼ cups all-purpose flour
2 tsp. lemon zest
  Yellow decorating sugar (optional)
1 8-oz. pkg. cream cheese, softened
⅔ cup butter, softened
3⅓ cups powdered sugar
1 Tbsp. lemon zest

1. For the cookies, in a large bowl beat shortening and ½ cup butter with a mixer on medium 30 seconds. Add granulated sugar, baking powder, and salt. Beat until combined. Beat in egg and vanilla. Beat in flour. Stir in 2 teaspoons lemon zest.

2. Divide dough in half. Shape each half into a 10-inch log. If desired, coat logs in decorating sugar. Wrap each in plastic wrap or waxed paper; chill until firm enough to slice (1 to 2 hours).

3. Preheat oven to 375°F. Use a serrated knife to cut logs into ⅛-inch slices; place 2 inches apart on ungreased cookie sheets. Bake 8 to 10 minutes or until set.

Cool on cookie sheets 1 minute. Remove; cool on a wire rack.

4. For the lemon-cream frosting, in a large bowl beat cream cheese and ⅔ cup butter with a mixer on medium until smooth. Gradually beat in powdered sugar until combined. Stir in lemon zest.

5. Spread lemon-cream frosting onto bottoms of half the cookies, using about 1 tablespoon for each cookie. Top with remaining cookies, bottom sides down. If desired, roll edges of sandwich cookies in additional granulated sugar. Chill 1 hour or until frosting is set. Makes 50 servings.

PER SERVING *140 cal., 8 g fat (4 g sat. fat), 20 mg chol., 76 mg sodium, 17 g carb., 0 g fiber, 12 g sugars, 1 g pro.*

CARROT CAKE OATMEAL CREAM PIES

PREP 45 minutes
CHILL 1 hour
BAKE 10 minutes per batch at 375°F

1   cup all-purpose flour
¾   tsp. ground cinnamon
½   tsp. baking soda
¼   tsp. salt
¼   tsp. ground allspice
¼   tsp. ground ginger
¾   cup butter, softened
½   cup granulated sugar
½   cup packed brown sugar
1   egg
2   tsp. vanilla
1   cup quick-cooking rolled oats
½   cup finely shredded carrot
⅓   cup raisins
4   oz. cream cheese, softened
2¼ to 2½ cups powdered sugar

1. In a medium bowl combine flour, cinnamon, soda, salt, allspice, and ginger. In a large bowl beat ½ cup butter and the sugars with a mixer on medium until combined. Beat in egg and 1 teaspoon vanilla. Beat in flour mixture. Stir in oats, carrot, and raisins. Cover and chill 1 hour or until dough is easy to handle.

2. Preheat oven to 375°F. Line two cookie sheets with parchment paper. Shape dough into 1-inch balls. Place 2 inches apart on prepared cookie sheets. Flatten cookies slightly with the bottom of a glass dipped in sugar.

3. Bake 10 to 12 minutes or until edges are set. Cool on cookie sheets 5 minutes. Remove; cool completely on a wire rack.

4. For filling, in a bowl beat together cream cheese and the remaining ¼ cup butter and 1 teaspoon vanilla until light and fluffy. Gradually add 1 cup powdered sugar, beating well. Gradually beat in enough remaining powdered sugar to reach spreading consistency.

5. Spread bottoms of half the cookies with cream cheese filling. Top with bottoms of remaining cookies. Makes 18 servings.

PER SERVING *250 cal., 10 g fat (6 g sat. fat), 37 mg chol., 156 mg sodium, 38 g carb., 1 g fiber, 28 g sugars, 2 g pro.*

CARROT CAKE
OATMEAL CREAM PIES

GINGERBREAD
CUTOUTS

GINGERBREAD CUTOUTS

PREP 50 minutes
CHILL 1 hour
BAKE 6 minutes per batch at 375°F

½   cup shortening
¼   cup butter, softened
½   cup granulated sugar
1   tsp. baking powder
1   tsp. ground ginger
½   tsp. baking soda
½   tsp. ground cinnamon
½   tsp. ground cloves
¼   tsp. salt
1   egg
½   cup molasses
1   Tbsp. cider vinegar
3   cups all-purpose flour

1. In a large bowl beat shortening and butter with a mixer on medium to high 30 seconds. Add sugar, baking powder, ginger, baking soda, cinnamon, cloves, and salt. Beat until combined, scraping bowl as needed. Beat in egg, molasses, and vinegar. Beat in as much of the flour as you can with the mixer. Stir in any remaining flour. Divide dough in half. Cover and chill 1 hour or until dough is easy to handle.
2. Preheat oven to 375°F. On a lightly floured surface, roll one dough portion and cut shapes using various cookie cutters, rerolling scraps as needed. Place cutouts 1 inch apart on ungreased cookie sheets.
3. Bake 6 to 8 minutes or until edges are firm. Cool on cookie sheets 1 minute. Remove; cool on a wire rack. Makes about 24 servings.
PER SERVING *151 cal., 7 g fat (2 g sat. fat), 13 mg chol., 92 mg sodium, 21 g carb., 0 g fiber, 9 g sugars, 2 g pro.*

CHOCOLATE-
ESPRESSO
CREAM SPRITZ

CHOCOLATE-ESPRESSO CREAM SPRITZ

PREP 40 minutes
BAKE 6 minutes per batch at 375°F

1½   cups butter, softened
½   of an 8-oz. pkg. cream cheese, softened
1   cup sugar
¼   cup unsweetened Dutch-process cocoa powder or unsweetened cocoa powder
1   tsp. baking powder
1   tsp. instant espresso coffee powder
1   egg
1   tsp. vanilla
3¼   cups all-purpose flour
     Finely chopped chocolate-covered espresso beans

1. Preheat oven to 375°F. In a large bowl beat butter and cream cheese with a mixer on medium to high 30 seconds. Add sugar, cocoa powder, baking powder, and espresso powder. Beat on medium until combined, scraping bowl as needed. Beat in egg and vanilla. Beat in as much of the flour as you can with the mixer. Stir in any remaining flour.
2. Force unchilled dough through a cookie press onto ungreased cookie sheets. Bake 6 minutes or until edges are firm. Remove; cool on wire racks. Sprinkle with chopped espresso beans. Makes 140 servings.
PER SERVING *45 cal., 3 g fat (2 g sat. fat), 7 mg chol., 23 mg sodium, 5 g carb., 0 g fiber, 2 g sugars, 1 g pro.*

CARAMEL SPRITZ

CLEMENTINE SPRITZ

CARAMEL SPRITZ

PREP 30 minutes
BAKE 6 minutes per batch at 375°F
STAND 30 minutes

1	cup granulated sugar
1½	cups butter, softened
1	tsp. baking powder
¼	tsp. salt
1	egg
1	tsp. vanilla
3½	cups all-purpose flour
1	recipe Caramel Drizzle

1. In an extra-large skillet heat granulated sugar over medium-high until sugar starts to melt. Reduce heat to medium-low. Stir unmelted sugar into melted sugar. When all sugar is melted and amber-color, pour onto a baking sheet lined with parchment; cool. Break sugar into pieces. Place sugar shards into a food processor. Process until fine.
2. Preheat oven to 375°F. In a large bowl beat butter with a mixer on medium to high 30 seconds. Add caramelized sugar, baking powder, and salt. Beat until combined, scraping bowl as needed. Beat in egg and vanilla. Beat in as much of the flour as you can with the mixer. Stir in any remaining flour.
3. Force unchilled dough through a cookie press* onto ungreased cookie sheets. Bake about 6 minutes or until edges are firm. Remove; cool on wire racks. Drizzle cooled cookies with Caramel Drizzle. Let stand until set. Makes 96 servings.

Caramel Drizzle In a small bowl stir together 1 cup powdered sugar, 2 tablespoons caramel ice cream topping, and 2 to 3 tablespoons milk until smooth and drizzling consistency. Makes ½ cup.

***Tip** Or, shape dough into 1¼-inch balls. Arrange 1 inch apart on ungreased cookie sheets. Flatten slightly. Bake, cool, and drizzle with icing as directed. Makes 64 servings.

PER SERVING 57 cal., 3 g fat (2 g sat. fat), 10 mg chol., 36 mg sodium, 7 g carb., 0 g fiber, 4 g sugars, 1 g pro.

CLEMENTINE SPRITZ

PREP 30 minutes
BAKE 7 minutes per batch at 375°F

1½	cups butter, softened
1½	cups granulated sugar
1	tsp. baking powder
1	egg
2	tsp. clementine zest
½	tsp. almond extract
3½	cups all-purpose flour
1	recipe Clementine Powdered Sugar Icing

1. Preheat oven to 375°F. In a large bowl beat butter with a mixer on medium 30 seconds. Add granulated sugar and baking powder; beat until combined, scraping bowl as needed. Beat in egg, clementine zest, and almond extract. Beat in flour.
2. Force unchilled dough through a cookie press onto ungreased cookie sheets. Bake 7 to 9 minutes or until edges are firm but not brown. Remove; cool on wire racks. Drizzle cookies with Clementine Powdered Sugar Icing; let stand until set. Makes 80 servings.

**Clementine Powdered Sugar
Icing** In a small bowl stir together
1½ cups powdered sugar, ½ teaspoon
clementine zest, and 2 tablespoons
clementine juice. If needed, stir in
additional clementine juice, 1 teaspoon
at a time, to reach drizzling consistency.
PER SERVING *75 cal., 4 g fat (2 g sat. fat),
11 mg chol., 35 mg sodium, 10 g carb.,
0 g fiber, 6 g sugars, 1 g pro.*

SKILLET GINGERBREAD COOKIE

PREP 20 minutes
BAKE 25 minutes at 350°F

1   cup all-purpose flour
1   tsp. ground ginger
½   tsp. baking soda
¼   tsp. ground cinnamon
¼   tsp. ground cloves
    Dash salt
⅓   cup shortening
½   cup granulated sugar
1   egg
2   Tbsp. molasses
1   recipe Lemon Icing

1. Preheat oven to 350°F. Butter bottom
and sides of an 8-inch cast-iron skillet
or two 6-inch cast-iron skillets. In a small
bowl stir together first six ingredients
(through salt).
2. In a medium bowl beat shortening
with a mixer on low 30 seconds.
Add sugar and beat until combined,
scraping bowl as needed. Beat in egg
and molasses. Beat in flour mixture.
Spread batter into prepared skillet(s).
3. Bake 25 minutes for large skillet, 18 to
20 minutes for small skillets, or until
center is set and top are light brown.
Cool slightly in skillet on a wire rack
(center may sink during cooling). Spread
Lemon Icing on warm cookie. Cut into
wedges or bars. Makes 24 servings.
Lemon Icing In a bowl stir together
1 cup powdered sugar, 1 teaspoon
lemon juice, and ½ teaspoon lemon
zest. Stir in enough milk for drizzling
consistency.
PER SERVING *73 cal., 4 g fat (1 g sat. fat),
9 mg chol., 40 mg sodium, 10 g carb.,
0 g fiber, 5 g sugars, 1 g pro.*

SKILLET
GINGERBREAD
COOKIE

LEMON-GINGER CHEESECAKE BALLS

PREP 25 minutes
CHILL 1 hour 15 minutes
FREEZE 15 minutes

2   8-oz. pkg. cream cheese, softened
1   cup powdered sugar
1   cup crushed gingersnaps (5 oz.)
2   Tbsp. heavy cream
1   Tbsp. finely chopped candied
    ginger
1   tsp. lemon zest

9   oz. bittersweet chocolate, chopped
1   Tbsp. shortening

1. In a large bowl beat cream cheese with a mixer on medium 30 seconds. Add powdered sugar, ½ cup of the crushed gingersnaps, the cream, ginger, and zest. Beat until combined. Cover and chill 1 hour or until dough is easy to handle.
2. Line a tray or rimmed baking sheet with waxed paper or parchment paper. Shape dough into 1-inch balls. Place on prepared tray. Freeze 15 minutes or until nearly firm.

3. In a small saucepan heat and stir chocolate and shortening over low until melted. Dip balls in chocolate to coat, allowing excess to drip off. Return to prepared tray. Sprinkle balls with remaining gingersnap crumbs before chocolate sets. Chill 15 minutes or until set. Refrigerate in an airtight container up to 2 weeks or freeze up to 3 months. Makes 46 servings.
PER SERVING 91 cal., 6 g fat (4 g sat. fat), 11 mg chol., 48 mg sodium, 9 g carb., 1 g fiber, 6 g sugars, 1 g pro.

LEMON-GINGER
CHEESECAKE BALLS

CRAN-PISTACHIO BALLS

PREP 25 minutes
CHILL 1 hour 30 minutes

⅓ cup butter
⅓ cup peanut butter
¼ cup light-color corn syrup
1½ cups regular or quick-cooking rolled oats
¼ cup chopped roasted, salted pistachios
¼ cup dried cranberries
1 tsp. orange zest
8 oz. white baking chocolate, melted

1. In a medium saucepan heat and stir butter, peanut butter, and corn syrup over medium until melted. Remove from heat.
2. Stir oats, pistachios, cranberries, and orange zest into peanut butter mixture. Cover and chill 1 to 2 hours or until firm enough to handle. Meanwhile, line a tray or rimmed baking sheet with parchment paper or waxed paper.
3. Shape oats mixture into 24 balls. Dip balls in melted white chocolate to coat, allowing excess to drip off. Place on prepared tray. If desired, sprinkle with additional chopped cranberries or finely chopped pistachios before chocolate sets. Chill 30 minutes or until set. Refrigerate in an airtight container up to 2 weeks or freeze up to 3 months. Makes 24 servings.

PER SERVING *125 cal., 8 g fat (4 g sat. fat), 9 mg chol., 47 mg sodium, 11 g carb., 1 g fiber, 7 g sugars, 2 g pro.*

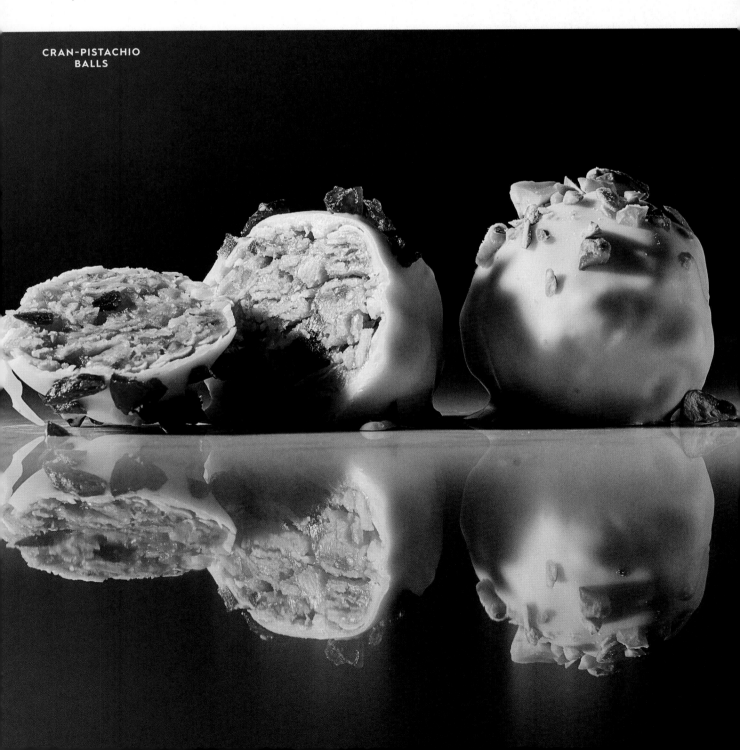

CRAN-PISTACHIO BALLS

LEMONY GLAZED SHORTBREAD BARS

LEMONY GLAZED SHORTBREAD BARS

PREP 40 minutes
BAKE 40 minutes at 300°F

3   cups all-purpose flour
⅓   cup cornstarch
1¼ cups powdered sugar
¼   cup lemon zest (5 to 6 lemons)
1½ cups butter, softened
1   Tbsp. lemon juice
½   tsp. salt
½   tsp. vanilla
1   recipe Lemony Glaze

1. Preheat oven to 300°F. Line a 13×9-inch baking pan with foil, extending foil over edges of pan. Lightly grease foil; set pan aside.
2. In a medium bowl stir together flour and cornstarch; set aside. In a small bowl combine powdered sugar and lemon zest. Pressing against side of bowl with a wooden spoon, work lemon zest into powdered sugar until sugar is yellow and fragrant.
3. In a large bowl beat butter, lemon juice, salt, and vanilla with a mixer on medium until combined. Gradually beat in sugar mixture. Stir in flour mixture.
4. Using lightly floured fingers, press dough into prepared pan. Bake 40 minutes or golden pale in color and edges start to brown. Remove from oven.
5. Immediately spoon Lemony Glaze over top, spreading gently to edges. Cool in pan on a wire rack. Using the edges of the foil, lift shortbread from pan. Cut into bars. Makes 32 servings.
Lemony Glaze In a bowl combine 2½ cups powdered sugar, 2 teaspoons lemon zest, 3 tablespoons lemon juice, 1 teaspoon light-color corn syrup, and ½ teaspoon vanilla. Whisk until smooth.
PER SERVING *181 cal., 9 g fat (5 g sat. fat), 23 mg chol., 98 mg sodium, 25 g carb., 0 g fiber, 14 g sugars, 1 g pro.*

ALMOND CRUNCH BARS

ALMOND CRUNCH BARS

PREP 30 minutes
CHILL 2 hours

30 vanilla creme sandwich cookies
¼   tsp. salt
½   cup butter, melted
1   12-oz. jar almond butter
2   cups powdered sugar
½   cup butter, softened
¼   cup heavy cream
½   cup chopped toasted almonds
6   oz. white baking chocolate, chopped
    Coarsely chopped red and green candy-coated milk chocolate-covered almonds

1. Line a 13×9-inch baking pan with foil, extending foil over edges of pan. For crust, in a food processor combine cookies and salt. Cover and process until crumbs form. Add melted butter. Cover and pulse just until combined. Press mixture evenly in bottom of prepared pan.
2. Reserve ⅓ cup almond butter. In a large bowl beat remaining almond butter, the powdered sugar, softened butter, and cream with a mixer on low to medium until smooth and fluffy. Stir in toasted almonds. Spread over crust in pan.
3. In a small saucepan heat and stir white chocolate and the reserved almond butter over low until smooth and melted. Spread over layers in pan. Sprinkle with candies.
4. Cover and chill at least 2 hours or until set. Use foil to lift almond crunch from pan. Cut into bars. Makes 48 servings.
PER SERVING *139 cal., 9 g fat (4 g sat. fat), 12 mg chol., 76 mg sodium, 13 g carb., 1 g fiber, 10 g sugars, 2 g pro.*

CINNAMON-WALNUT CRACKER BARS

PREP 20 minutes
CHILL 4 hours

- 80 rich rectangular crackers (2 sleeves)
- ¾ cup butter
- ¾ cup packed brown sugar
- ¼ cup milk
- 1 tsp. ground cinnamon
- 1 egg, lightly beaten
- 1 cup chopped toasted walnuts
- 4 oz. bittersweet chocolate, melted
  Grated milk chocolate or bittersweet chocolate (optional)

1. Line a 9-inch square baking pan with foil, extending foil over edges. Line bottom of pan with some of the crackers, breaking to fit. Reserve the same number of whole crackers for top as for bottom. Finely crush remaining crackers (about 1 cup).

2. In a medium saucepan combine butter, brown sugar, milk, cinnamon, and egg. Cook and stir constantly over medium just until mixture is bubbly. Remove from heat. Stir in walnuts and crushed crackers. Cool slightly.

3. Spoon walnut mixture over crackers in pan; carefully spread evenly. Place reserved whole crackers on top. Spread melted bittersweet chocolate over top crackers. If desired, sprinkle with grated chocolate. Cover and chill at least 4 hours or until firm. Use foil to lift out crackers. Cut into bars. Makes 36 servings.

PER SERVING 130 cal., 9 g fat (4 g sat. fat), 16 mg chol., 104 mg sodium, 12 g carb., 1 g fiber, 6 g sugars, 1 g pro.

CINNAMON-WALNUT CRACKER BARS

FUDGE RIPPLE PECAN BROWNIES

PREP 30 minutes
BAKE 30 minutes at 350°F
STAND 2 hours

- ½ cup butter
- 3 oz. unsweetened chocolate, coarsely chopped
- 1 cup sugar
- 2 eggs
- 1 tsp. vanilla
- ⅔ cup all-purpose flour
- ¼ tsp. baking soda
- 1 cup chopped pecans, toasted (tip, page 24)
- ¾ cup semisweet chocolate pieces
- 20 vanilla caramels, unwrapped
- 1 Tbsp. milk

1. In a medium saucepan heat and stir butter and unsweetened chocolate over low until melted and smooth. Remove from heat. Cool.

2. Meanwhile, preheat oven to 350°F. Line an 8-inch square baking pan with foil, extending the foil about 1 inch beyond edges of pan. Grease foil; set pan aside.

3. Stir sugar into cooled chocolate mixture in saucepan. Add eggs, one at a time, beating with a wooden spoon after each addition just until combined. Stir in vanilla. In a small bowl stir together flour and baking soda. Add flour mixture to chocolate mixture, stirring just until combined. Stir in ½ cup pecans and ½ cup chocolate pieces. Spread batter in prepared pan.

4. Bake 30 minutes. Cool in pan on a wire rack.

5. Meanwhile, in a small saucepan heat and stir caramels and milk over medium-low until melted and smooth. Spread caramel over cooled brownies. Sprinkle with remaining ½ cup pecans.

6. In a small saucepan heat and stir the remaining ¼ cup chocolate pieces over low until melted and smooth. Drizzle chocolate over brownies. Let stand 2 hours before serving.

7. Using the edges of the foil, lift brownies out of pan; cut into bars. Makes 25 servings.

PER SERVING 191 cal., 12 g fat (5 g sat. fat), 25 mg chol., 68 mg sodium, 21 g carb., 1 g fiber, 14 g sugars, 2 g pro.

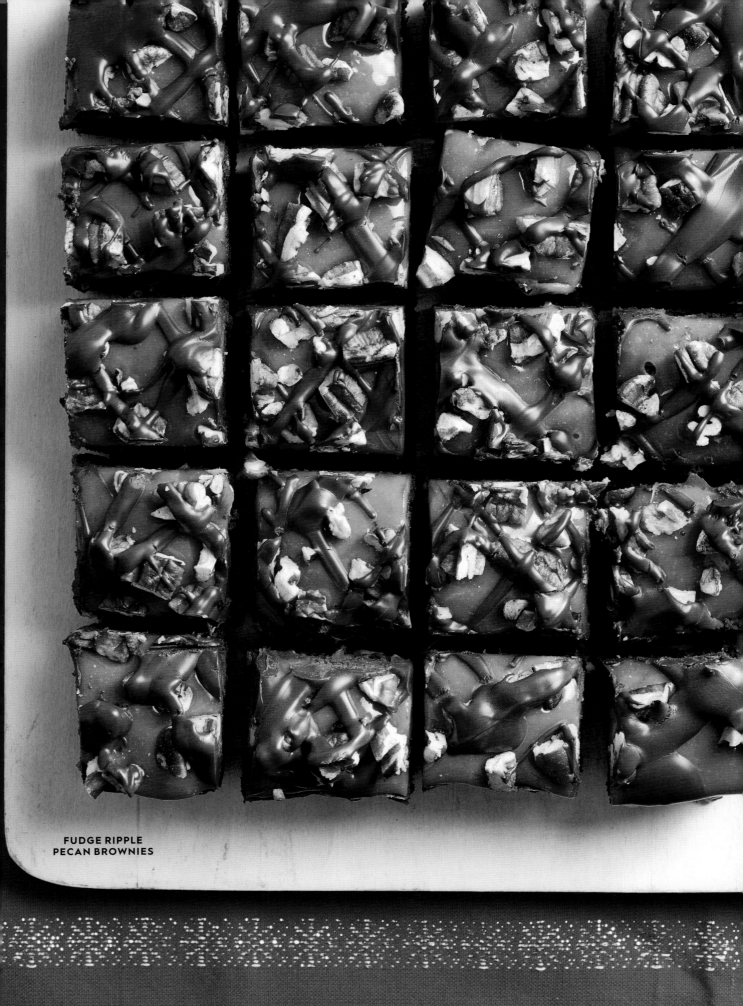

FUDGE RIPPLE
PECAN BROWNIES

Tasteful Gifts

Share your appreciation of others with homemade treats to deliver throughout the season.

PRETZEL SNOW
PEOPLE; PAGE 124

CARAMEL CRACKER
CANDY, PAGE 127

KITTY'S CATNIP
CHRISTMAS COOKIES

KITTY'S CATNIP CHRISTMAS COOKIES

PREP 45 minutes
BAKE 20 minutes at 350°F

1	6-oz. can tuna (water-pack)
	Chicken broth or fat-free milk (optional)
2	Tbsp. canola oil
1	to 2 Tbsp. dried catnip, crushed
1	cup all-purpose flour
½	cup whole wheat flour
½	cup shredded cheddar cheese (2 oz.)
	Water (optional)

1. Preheat oven to 350°F. Line two large cookie sheets with foil. Drain tuna, reserving ¼ cup liquid (if needed, add broth to equal ¼ cup). In a small bowl combine tuna, the ¼ cup liquid, oil, and catnip. In a medium bowl stir together both flours. Stir in tuna mixture and cheese just until combined. If needed, stir in up to 2 tablespoons water to moisten dough. Shape into a ball.
2. On a lightly floured surface, roll dough into an ⅛-inch-thick rectangle; trim and discard uneven edges. Using a pizza cutter or sharp knife, cut rectangle into ½-inch squares. Place squares on prepared cookie sheets.
3. Bake on separate oven racks 20 to 25 minutes or until cookies are still somewhat soft, rotating sheets halfway through baking. Cool on cookie sheets. Makes 80 servings.
PER SERVING *16 cal., 1 g fat (0 g sat. fat), 1 mg chol., 11 mg sodium, 2 g carb., 0 g fiber, 0 g sugars, 1 g pro.*

As a Gift Decorate a take-away box. From cardstock, cut triangles for ears and strips for whiskers. Hot-glue ears to one open flap, and trim around ears. Glue whiskers and a pom-pom nose to box. Fill a bag with crackers, place in box, and tape undecorated flaps closed. Attach instructions: Refrigerate crackers up to 1 week or freeze up to 6 months.

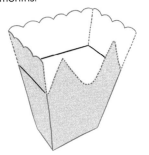

SPICED PUMPKIN SNAPS DOG TREATS

SPICED PUMPKIN SNAPS DOG TREATS

PREP 30 minutes
BAKE 45 minutes at 300°F
STAND 8 hours

1	cup natural apple juice
1	cup canned pumpkin
¼	cup honey
2	Tbsp. canola oil
1¼	cups rolled oats
⅓	cup wheat germ
1	cup whole wheat flour
1	tsp. ground cinnamon
1½	cups all-purpose flour

1. Preheat oven to 300°F. Line two large cookie sheets with parchment paper. In a large saucepan heat and stir apple juice, pumpkin, honey, and oil until mixture is simmering. Remove from heat. Stir in oats and wheat germ; cool slightly. Stir in whole wheat flour and cinnamon. Stir in all-purpose flour. Divide dough in half.
2. On a lightly floured surface, roll one portion of dough at a time into a 10-inch square. Using a pastry wheel or knife, cut dough into 2-inch squares. Place squares close together on prepared cookie sheets.
3. Bake on separate oven racks 45 minutes, rotating sheets halfway through baking. Turn off oven; let dry overnight. Makes 50 servings.
PER SERVING *46 cal., 1 g fat (0 g sat. fat), 0 mg chol., 1 mg sodium, 9 g carb., 1 g fiber, 2 g sugars, 1 g pro.*

As a Gift Draw a stocking pattern with cuff on paper. Place crepe paper, design down, on plain paper. Trace and cut out stocking. Hot-glue stocking edges together, leaving cuff edges and top open. Let dry. Turn cuff over stocking; punch hole in heel side of cuff, and tie on a tag. Fill stocking with treats; include instructions. Refrigerate up to 1 week.

SPICY BLACK BEAN
AND CORN SOUP MIX

SPICY BLACK BEAN AND CORN SOUP MIX

START TO FINISH 15 minutes

2	Tbsp. dried parsley
2	Tbsp. chili powder
2	tsp. dried oregano
1	tsp. granulated garlic or garlic powder
1	tsp. ground cumin
1	tsp. ground coriander
1	tsp. black pepper
2	cups dried corn
½	cup dried chopped green and/or red sweet pepper or dried corn
¼	cup instant chicken bouillon powder
¼	cup dried minced onion
2	bay leaves
3	cups dried black beans

1. For seasoning mix, in a small bowl stir together first seven ingredients (through black pepper).

2. In two quart-size glass jars (or cellophane bags) layer dried corn, sweet pepper, bouillon powder, onion, and half the seasoning mix. Top with 1 bay leaf in each. Divide beans between two resealable plastic bags; seal bags and place in jars. Seal jars. Store in a cool, dry place up to 6 months. Makes 16 servings.

To Make Soup Remove beans from one jar. Rinse beans; drain. In a large saucepan combine beans and 6 cups water. Bring to boiling; reduce heat. Simmer, uncovered, 2 minutes. Remove from heat. Cover and let stand 1 hour. Drain and rinse beans. In a 5- to 6-quart slow cooker combine beans, remaining soup mix, and 8 cups fresh water. Cover and cook on low 9 to 10 hours or high 4½ to 5 hours or until beans are tender. If desired, top servings with shredded cheddar cheese, sour cream, and/or fresh cilantro and serve with lime wedges. Makes 8 servings.

PER SERVING *186 cal., 1 g fat (0 g sat. fat), 0 mg chol., 587 mg sodium, 35 g carb., 7 g fiber, 3 g sugars, 9 g pro.*

As a Gift Cut out jar topper from paper or fabric. Attach to jars with twine or ribbon. Print a label of ingredients and instructions on sticker paper. Cut out and press to jars.

SPICY
**BLACK BEAN
+ CORN** SOUP MIX

Remove beans from soup mix. Rinse beans; drain. In a large saucepan combine beans and 6 cups water. Bring to boiling; reduce heat. Simmer, uncovered, 2 minutes. Remove from heat. Cover and let stand 1 hour. Drain and rinse beans. In a 5- to 6-qt. slow cooker combine beans, remaining soup mix, and 8 cups fresh water. Cover and cook on low 9 to 10 hours or high 4½ to 5 hours or until beans are tender. If desired, serve with lime wedges.

RANCH POTATO CHIP SNACK MIX

PREP 15 minutes
BAKE 25 minutes at 325°F

- 3 cups kettle-style potato chips
- 2 cups sweet potato chips
- 2 cups garlic-flavor rye chips
- 3 cups pretzel sticks or mini pretzel twists
- 1 cup mixed nuts
- ½ cup butter, melted
- 1 1-oz. pkg. ranch dry salad dressing mix

1. Preheat oven to 325°F. Line a shallow roasting pan with foil, extending foil over edges. In prepared pan combine potato chips, sweet potato chips, and rye chips. Bake 5 minutes. Stir in pretzels and nuts. Drizzle with melted butter and sprinkle with salad dressing mix; toss to coat.

2. Bake 10 minutes; stir. Bake 10 minutes more or until lightly toasted. Using foil, lift out snack mix; cool on foil. Store in an airtight container at room temperature up to 1 week. Makes 24 servings.

PER SERVING *148 cal., 11 g fat (4 g sat. fat), 10 mg chol., 437 mg sodium, 11 g carb., 1 g fiber, 1 g sugars, 2 g pro.*

As a Gift For snack cups, print tags onto sticker paper. Color with markers, if desired. Adhere tags to paper cups. Place a transparent treat bag in cup, fill with snack mix, and seal bag. For treat bags, decorate paper bags with paint or markers. Print tags onto sticker paper; cut out and color with markers, if desired, and adhere to bags. Fold a cuff in top of bag. Place transparent bags in treat bags, fill with snack mix, and seal.

RANCH POTATO CHIP SNACK MIX

CINNAMON-SUGAR
BOURBON-
PUMPKIN MUFFINS

CINNAMON-SUGAR BOURBON-PUMPKIN MUFFINS

PREP 25 minutes
BAKE 25 minutes at 350°F
COOL 10 minutes

3⅓ cups granulated sugar
¾ cup finely chopped pecans
2 tsp. ground cinnamon
2¾ cups all-purpose flour
2 tsp. baking soda
1 tsp. salt
1 15-oz. can pumpkin
¾ cup vegetable oil
3 eggs
¼ cup bourbon or water
1 recipe Bourbon Icing (optional)

1. Preheat oven to 350°F. Line twenty-four 2½-inch muffin cups with paper bake cups. In a small bowl combine ⅔ cup granulated sugar, the pecans, and 1 teaspoon cinnamon. In an extra-large bowl stir together flour, baking soda, salt, and remaining 1 teaspoon cinnamon. Make a well in center of flour mixture.

2. In a large bowl whisk together remaining 2⅔ cups granulated sugar, the pumpkin, oil, eggs, and bourbon. Add egg mixture all at once to flour mixture. Stir just until moistened (batter should be lumpy). Spoon batter into prepared muffin cups, filling each three-fourths full. Sprinkle with pecan mixture.

3. Bake 25 to 28 minutes or until a toothpick inserted near center comes out clean. Cool in muffin cups on wire racks 10 minutes. Remove; cool on wire racks. If desired, drizzle with Bourbon Icing before serving. Makes 24 servings.

PER SERVING *265 cal., 10 g fat (1 g sat. fat), 23 mg chol., 212 mg sodium, 41 g carb., 1 g fiber, 29 g sugars, 3 g pro.*

Bourbon Icing In a bowl stir together 1 cup powdered sugar, 1 tablespoon bourbon, and enough milk (2 to 3 teaspoons) to reach drizzling consistency.

As a Gift Fold paper plate as indicated by gray lines. Cut plate as indicated by red lines. Fold up sides and secure corners with tape or hot glue. If desired, wrap muffins in plastic wrap and place on tray. Wrap with ribbon. Attach a tag.

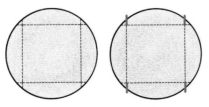

CRANBERRY-PEAR SCONES

PREP 25 minutes
BAKE 20 minutes at 400°F

2¾ cups all-purpose flour
½   cup granulated sugar
1   Tbsp. baking powder
½   tsp. salt
½   cup butter, cut up
1   cup fresh or frozen cranberries
½   cup finely chopped pear
½   cup chopped walnuts
2   eggs, lightly beaten
¾   cup heavy cream
1   tsp. vanilla bean paste
     Coarse sugar
1   recipe Maple Butter

1. Preheat oven to 400°F. Line an extra-large baking sheet with parchment paper. In a large bowl stir together flour, granulated sugar, baking powder, and salt. Using a pastry blender, cut in butter until mixture resembles coarse crumbs. Stir in cranberries, pear, and walnuts. Make a well in center of flour mixture.
2. In a small bowl combine eggs, cream, and vanilla bean paste. Add egg mixture all at once to flour mixture. Using a fork, stir just until moistened.
3. Turn dough out onto a lightly floured surface. Knead dough by folding and gently pressing it 10 to 12 strokes or until nearly smooth. Divide in half. Pat or lightly roll each dough half into a 6-inch circle. Cut each circle into six wedges.

4. Place wedges 2 inches apart on prepared baking sheet. Brush with additional cream and sprinkle with coarse sugar. Bake 20 minutes or until bottoms are golden. Remove; cool on a wire rack. Package with Maple Butter. Makes 12 servings.
Maple Butter In a small bowl beat together ½ cup softened butter, 3 tablespoons pure maple syrup, and ¼ teaspoon vanilla bean paste until smooth. Makes ½ cup.
PER SERVING *392 cal., 25 g fat (14 g sat. fat), 89 mg chol., 358 mg sodium, 38 g carb., 2 g fiber, 14 g sugars, 5 g pro.*
As a Gift Fill bag with scones. Fold over top, layer with a strip of cardstock, and secure with a clothespin "tree."

CRANBERRY-PEAR SCONES

PEANUT BUTTER BALL ORNAMENTS

Crispy Peanut Butter Balls Prepare as directed, except stir 1 cup crisp rice cereal into peanut butter mixture before shaping into balls. Makes 40 servings.
To Store Place ornaments in a single layer in an airtight container. Refrigerate up to 1 month or freeze up to 3 months. If frozen, thaw at room temperature before serving.
PER SERVING *167 cal., 10 g fat (5 g sat. fat), 5 mg chol., 64 mg sodium, 18 g carb., 1 g fiber, 16 g sugars, 2 g pro.*
As a Gift Line a mini loaf pan with decorative waxed paper. Arrange ornaments. Tie on ribbon, gift tag, and storage directions (above).

PRETZEL SNOW PEOPLE

PREP 40 minutes
STAND 30 minutes

12	oz. vanilla-flavor candy coating (almond bark), coarsely chopped
1	tsp. shortening
18	pretzel rods
	Coarse sugar
	Candies, sprinkles, and/or icing and rolled fruit leather

1. Line a large cookie sheet with waxed paper. In a small heavy saucepan cook and stir vanilla coating and shortening over low until melted and smooth.
2. Spoon melted white coating over three-fourths of each pretzel rod, turning pretzel to coat and allowing excess coating to drip off. Sprinkle with sugar. Place coated pretzels on waxed paper. Let stand 30 minutes or until set.
3. Decorate as snow people using candies, sprinkles, and/or icing for faces and fruit leather for scarves. Makes 18 servings.
To Store Layer coated pretzels between waxed paper in an airtight container. Store at room temperature up to 3 days or refrigerate up to 1 week.
PER SERVING *185 cal., 8 g fat (6 g sat. fat), 0 mg chol., 150 mg sodium, 25 g carb., 0 g fiber, 19 g sugars, 1 g pro.*
As a Gift Make a tag on sticker paper. Adhere to a french fry box, fill box with pretzels, and place box in a clear treat bag. Tie with ribbon.

PEANUT BUTTER BALL ORNAMENTS

PREP 40 minutes
STAND 10 minutes

1	cup peanut butter
6	Tbsp. butter, softened
2	cups powdered sugar
12	oz. white, red, and/or green candy coating
	Miniature chocolate-covered peanut butter cups

1. Line a tray or baking sheet with waxed paper. In a large bowl stir together peanut butter and butter. Gradually add powdered sugar, stirring until combined. If necessary, knead with hands until smooth. Shape into 1-inch balls; place on prepared tray.
2. In separate bowls microwave candy coating, one color at a time, according to package directions until melted; stir until smooth. Using a fork, dip peanut butter balls, one at a time, into melted coating, allowing excess coating to drip off. Return to waxed paper; let stand 10 minutes or until set.
3. Fill heavy resealable plastic bags with additional melted candy coating. Snip a small hole in one corner of each bag. Pipe coating onto coated balls to create drizzles, dots, or other designs. Pipe a dot of coating on top of each ball and add a peanut butter cup, pressing to adhere. Let stand until coating is set. Makes 40 servings.

PRETZEL SNOW PEOPLE

CARAMEL
CRACKER CANDY

CARAMEL CRACKER CANDY

PREP 15 minutes
BAKE 8 minutes at 350°F
STAND 5 minutes
COOL 30 minutes
CHILL 1 hour

11	or 12 graham crackers
½	cup butter
⅓	cup packed brown sugar
½	tsp. ground cinnamon or pumpkin pie spice
¼	tsp. salt
1	tsp. vanilla
2	cups milk chocolate or white baking chips
¼	to ½ cup toppings, such as sprinkles, almond-toffee bits, chopped or finely chopped toasted nuts, or chopped dried tart cherries, cranberries, or apricots

1. Preheat oven to 350°F. Line a 15×10-inch baking pan with foil, extending foil over edges. Cover bottom of prepared pan with graham crackers, breaking to fit or overlapping as needed.
2. In a medium saucepan bring butter, brown sugar, cinnamon, and salt to boiling, stirring to melt butter. Boil gently, without stirring, 2 minutes. Remove from heat. Stir in vanilla.
3. Spread butter mixture over crackers. Bake 8 to 10 minutes or until bubbly. Place pan on a wire rack. Sprinkle with chocolate chips; let stand 5 minutes to soften.
4. Spread softened chocolate on crackers and sprinkle with toppings. Cool 30 minutes. Chill 1 hour or until chocolate is set. Using foil, lift out candy. Break into irregular pieces. Makes 24 servings.
PER SERVING *182 cal., 11 g fat (7 g sat. fat), 17 mg chol., 103 mg sodium, 20 g carb., 1 g fiber, 16 g sugars, 2 g pro.*
As a Gift Decorate a generous-size treat box with pom-poms or holiday designs. Line the box with tissue paper to extend well over top of box. Fill with large "shards" of Carmel Cracker Candy.

COOKIE TRUFFLES

PREP 20 minutes
CHILL 30 minutes

1	11.3-oz. pkg. pecan shortbread, such as Keebler
½	cup mascarpone cheese
8	oz. vanilla- or chocolate-flavor candy coating (almond bark), chopped
	Finely chopped pecans

1. Line a tray or baking sheet with waxed paper. Place shortbread in a food processor; cover and pulse until fine crumbs form.* Add cheese; cover and pulse until mixture comes together.
2. Using a cookie scoop, drop 1¼-inch mounds onto prepared tray. Shape into balls. Chill at least 30 minutes.
3. In a medium bowl microwave candy coating 1 to 2 minutes or until melted and smooth, stirring twice.
4. Using a fork, dip each ball into melted coating, allowing excess to drip off. Return to prepared tray. Top with pecans while wet; let stand until set. Makes 29 servings.
*Note Or place shortbread in a resealable plastic bag and finely crush with a rolling pin. Transfer crumbs to a large bowl and stir in cheese until combined.
To Store Place truffles in a single layer in an airtight container. Refrigerate up to 2 weeks or freeze up to 3 months.
PER SERVING *103 cal., 7 g fat (3 g sat. fat), 6 mg chol., 45 mg sodium, 10 g carb., 0 g fiber, 5 g sugars, 1 g pro.*
As a Gift Paint a white paper ice cream pint container or paper cup with acrylic paint. Let dry. Fill with truffles. Cut 1-inch slits in top and fold down tabs to close. Secure with ribbon. Attach storage directions (above).

COOKIE TRUFFLES

New Year's Eve Party

Top off the holiday season with a festive feast for friends and family.

WINTER PEAR SALAD,
PAGE 141

GRAPEFRUIT TART WITH CHOCOLATE-ALMOND CRUST, PAGE 142

POMEGRANATE SPRITZERS

FRENCH 75

PER SERVING *84 cal., 0 g fat, 0 mg chol., 3 mg sodium, 7 g carb., 0 g fiber, 4 g sugars, 0 g pro.*
Nonalcoholic Pomegranate Sparkler Prepare as directed, except substitute sparkling apple juice for the champagne.

GOUGÈRES

PREP 30 minutes
COOL 10 minutes
FREEZE 1 hour
BAKE 25 minutes per batch at 400°F

1½ cups water
½   cup butter, cut into pieces
¼   tsp. salt
1½ cups all-purpose flour
5   eggs
1½ cups shredded Gruyère cheese (6 oz.)
1   Tbsp. Dijon mustard
⅛   tsp. cayenne pepper

1. Line two baking sheets with parchment paper. In a large saucepan bring the water, butter, and salt to boiling. Immediately add flour all at once; stir vigorously. Cook and stir until mixture forms a ball. Remove from heat. Cool 10 minutes. Add eggs, one at a time, stirring after each addition until smooth. Stir in cheese, mustard, and cayenne pepper.
2. Using a pastry bag fitted with a ½-inch star tip, pipe batter into 1-inch mounds close together on prepared baking sheets. (Or use a small cookie scoop to drop batter into 1¼-inch mounds.) Freeze 1 to 2 hours or until firm.
3. Preheat oven to 400°F. Bake 25 minutes or until puffed and golden. Serve warm. Makes 72 servings.
PER SERVING *37 cal., 3 g fat (1 g sat. fat), 19 mg chol., 48 mg sodium, 2 g carb., 0 g fiber, 0 g sugars, 2 g pro.*

FRENCH 75

START TO FINISH 5 minutes

    Cracked ice
2   oz. gin
1   tsp. simple syrup*
1   Tbsp. fresh lemon juice
5   oz. chilled brut champagne
    Lemon twist (optional)

1. In a chilled cocktail shaker combine ice, gin, simple syrup, and lemon juice. Shake well. Fill a chilled champagne flute half-full of ice, then strain cocktail into glass. Top with champagne and, if desired, garnish with a lemon twist. Makes 1 serving.
PER SERVING *250 cal., 0 g fat, 0 mg chol., 9 mg sodium, 4 g carb., 0 g fiber, 10 g sugars, 0 g pro.*
*Simple syrup In a saucepan bring equal amounts of water and sugar to boiling, stirring constantly, until sugar is dissolved. Simmer 5 minutes; cool completely. Store syrup in an airtight glass jar up to 3 months.

POMEGRANATE SPRITZERS

START TO FINISH 5 minutes

1   cup pomegranate juice, chilled
1   750-milliliter bottle champagne or sparkling wine, chilled
    Pomegranate seeds (optional)*

1. Add 2 tablespoons pomegranate juice to each of eight champagne flutes. Pour champagne into each glass to serve. If desired, add a few pomegranate seeds to each glass. Makes 8 servings.
*Tip To separate seeds from a fresh pomegranate, score an X in the top of a pomegranate. Break apart into quarters. Working in a bowl of cool water, immerse each quarter; use your fingers to loosen seeds from white membrane. Discard peel and membrane. Drain seeds. Cover and chill up to 24 hours.

GOUGÈRES

TOASTED WILD RICE
GRIDDLE CAKES

TOASTED WILD RICE GRIDDLE CAKES

PREP 20 minutes
COOK 46 minutes plus 5 minutes per batch for griddle cakes
COOL 10 minutes

2   cups water
1   cup wild rice, rinsed and drained
3   Tbsp. butter
1   tsp. salt
¼   tsp. crushed red pepper
¾   cup finely chopped fennel
½   cup finely chopped red onion
½   cup coarsely shredded carrot
1¼   cups soft bread crumbs
⅓   cup grated Parmesan cheese
2   eggs, lightly beaten
2   Tbsp. canola oil
¼   cup sour cream
1   tsp. Dijon mustard
     Microgreens (optional)

1. In a medium-size heavy saucepan bring the water to boiling. Stir in rice; reduce heat. Simmer, covered, 40 to 50 minutes or just until rice begins to split; drain.

2. Add butter, salt, and crushed red pepper to rice in saucepan. Cook and stir over medium-high 6 minutes or until rice is toasted and has a nutty aroma. Stir in fennel, onion, and carrot. Remove from heat. Stir in bread crumbs and cheese; cool 10 minutes. Stir in eggs until combined. If desired, cover and chill up to 6 hours. Stir before using.

3. For griddle cakes, in an extra-large skillet heat oil over medium-high. Add batter, using 3 tablespoons for each cake; spread to 3 inches. Cook 3 to 4 minutes or until bottoms are crisp and browned. Turn and cook 2 to 3 minutes more or until bottoms are browned. Keep warm in a 200°F oven while cooking remaining cakes, adding additional oil as needed.

4. In a small bowl combine sour cream and mustard. Serve griddle cakes with sour cream and, if desired, top with microgreens. Makes 18 servings.

PER SERVING *94 cal., 5 g fat (2 g sat. fat), 29 mg chol., 207 mg sodium, 10 g carb., 1 g fiber, 1 g sugars, 3 g pro.*

SPINACH PHYLLO TRIANGLES

SPINACH PHYLLO TRIANGLES

PREP 50 minutes
FREEZE 1 hour
BAKE 15 minutes per batch at 375°F

1   10-oz. pkg. frozen chopped spinach, thawed and well drained
½   cup finely chopped onion
1   clove garlic, minced
1½   cups finely crumbled feta cheese (6 oz.)
½   tsp. dried oregano, crushed
24   sheets frozen phyllo dough (14×9-inch rectangles), thawed
½   cup butter, melted

1. For filling, cook spinach, onion, and garlic according to spinach package directions. Drain well. In a medium bowl combine spinach mixture, cheese, and oregano.

2. Line a large baking sheet with waxed paper. Unfold phyllo dough; remove one sheet. (Keep remaining phyllo covered with plastic wrap to prevent it from drying out.) Lightly brush sheet with some of the melted butter. Place another phyllo sheet on top; brush with butter.

3. Cut the two layered sheets lengthwise for three 3×14-inch strips. For each triangle, spoon a well-rounded teaspoon of filling 1 inch from an end of strip. Fold narrow end of strip over filling to align with long edge; continue folding to completely enclose filling. Place on prepared baking sheet. Continue with phyllo, butter, and filling to make 36 triangles. Freeze 1 hour or until firm. (To make ahead, transfer to freezer containers; freeze up to 2 months.)

4. To serve, preheat oven to 375°F. Place frozen triangles on a baking sheet; brush with additional melted butter. Bake 15 minutes or until golden. Serve warm. Makes 18 servings.

PER SERVING *162 cal., 9 g fat (5 g sat. fat), 25 mg chol., 321 mg sodium, 15 g carb., 1 g fiber, 1 g sugars, 4 g pro.*

borders around vegetables, pleating as necessary. Sprinkle vegetables with remaining ¼ cup goat cheese.
5. Roast 20 minutes or until tarts are golden brown, rotating pans after 10 minutes. Drizzle with remaining oil and top with rosemary sprigs. Makes 8 servings.
PER SERVING *479 cal., 31 g fat (11 g sat. fat), 24 mg chol., 517 mg sodium, 43 g carb., 3 g fiber, 6 g sugars, 7 g pro.*

BUTTERED FETTUCCINE WITH BRUSSELS SPROUTS AND PARMESAN

START TO FINISH 30 minutes

12	oz. dried fettuccine
½	cup butter
3	cups fresh Brussels sprouts, trimmed and quartered
2	tsp. lemon zest
1½	tsp. chopped fresh thyme
½	cup finely grated Parmesan cheese, plus extra for garnish
	Freshly ground black pepper

1. In a large saucepan cook fettuccine in boiling, well-salted water according to package directions until al dente. Drain pasta, reserving 1½ cups pasta water for sauce.
2. In an extra-large skillet melt 2 tablespoons butter over medium. Add Brussels sprouts; cook 8 to 10 minutes, stirring occasionally, until browned and tender. Remove sprouts from skillet.
3. Add remaining butter to skillet. Stir in 1 cup reserved pasta water, the lemon zest, and thyme. Bring just to boiling.
4. Add cooked pasta, Brussels sprouts, and Parmesan to skillet. Toss with tongs until thoroughly coated, adding additional pasta water as needed to loosen the sauce. Season with pepper; serve with additional grated Parmesan, if desired. Makes 6 servings.
PER SERVING *383 cal., 18 g fat (11 g sat. fat), 46 mg chol., 253 mg sodium, 47 g carb., 4 g fiber, 3 g sugars, 11 g pro.*

RUSTIC WINTER VEGETABLE TARTS

RUSTIC WINTER VEGETABLE TARTS

PREP 25 minutes
ROAST 55 minutes at 425°F

7½	cups winter vegetables (such as winter squash, sweet potatoes, red onion, parsnips, carrots, turnips, and rutabagas), peeled and seeded as necessary and cut into bite-size chunks
4	slices thick-cut bacon, cut into 1-inch pieces
3	Tbsp. olive oil
2	Tbsp. chopped fresh thyme leaves
¼	tsp. salt
¼	tsp. black pepper
1	15-oz. pkg. rolled refrigerated unbaked pie crust (2 crusts)
1	cup crumbled chèvre (4-oz.)
1	Tbsp. balsamic vinegar
4	cloves garlic, minced
	Fresh rosemary sprigs

1. In large bowl toss prepared vegetables with bacon, 2 tablespoons oil, the thyme, salt, and pepper. Spread in a 15×10-inch baking pan. Place pan on lowest oven rack of cold oven; turn oven to 425°F. Roast 35 minutes, stirring every 10 minutes, until vegetables are golden and tender.
2. Meanwhile, roll each pie crust into a 12-inch square. Cut each square into four squares; divide between two parchment-lined baking sheets.
3. Remove vegetables from oven; stir in ¾ cup cheese, the vinegar, and garlic. Leave oven on; adjust racks to lower center and upper positions.
4. Divide vegetable mixture among dough, leaving 1-inch borders. Fold

BUTTERED FETTUCCINE
WITH BRUSSELS SPROUTS
AND PARMESAN

COLD ROASTED SALMON

COLD ROASTED SALMON

PREP 30 minutes
ROAST 15 minutes at 475°F
CHILL 4 hours

    Olive oil
6 6-oz. center-cut salmon fillets, skinned
2 Tbsp. peppercorn or tarragon mustard
3 slices bacon, crisp-cooked, drained, and halved
3 oz. goat cheese (chèvre), crumbled
    Snipped fresh chives (optional)

1. Preheat oven to 475°F. Lightly oil a 15×10-inch baking pan with olive oil. Arrange salmon fillets in prepared pan. Turn under any thin portions of fillets to make uniform thickness. Spread mustard over tops of fillets.
2. Roast 15 to 18 minutes or until fish flakes easily when tested with a fork. Transfer to plate; cover and chill at least 4 hours or up to 24 hours.
3. To serve, arrange salmon on a serving dish; top with bacon, goat cheese, and, if desired, chives. Makes 6 servings.
PER SERVING *407 cal., 26 g fat (8 g sat. fat), 118 mg chol., 387 mg sodium, 1 g carb., 0 g fiber, 0 g sugars, 40 g pro.*

PORK TENDERLOIN WITH GREEN OLIVE TAPENADE

PREP 40 minutes
GRILL 35 minutes
STAND 10 minutes

1 cup pitted green olives
1 Tbsp. drained capers
1 Tbsp. Dijon mustard
1 Tbsp. olive oil
1 Tbsp. lemon juice
2 tsp. anchovy paste
1 tsp. snipped fresh thyme
1 clove garlic, minced
2 12- to 16-oz. pork tenderloins

1. For tapenade, in a food processor or blender combine olives, capers, mustard, oil, lemon juice, anchovy paste, thyme, and garlic. Cover and process until nearly smooth, scraping down sides as necessary. If desired, cover and chill up to 24 hours.

PORK TENDERLOIN WITH GREEN OLIVE TAPENADE

2. Trim fat from tenderloins. Make a lengthwise cut along the center of each tenderloin, cutting almost to, but not through, opposite side. Spread meat open. Place tenderloins between two pieces of plastic wrap; lightly pound meat with the flat side of a meat mallet. Overlap tenderloins about 2 inches along one long side. Lightly round meat into a 12×10-inch rectangle. Remove plastic wrap.
3. Spread tapenade over meat to within 1 inch of edges. Fold in long sides just to cover edge of tapenade. Starting at one short side, roll up meat. To secure, tie at 1-inch intervals with 100%-cotton kitchen string.

4. Grill meat over medium indirect heat 35 to 40 minutes or until an instant-read thermometer inserted in meat registers 145°F.
5. Remove meat from grill. Cover with foil; let stand 10 minutes before slicing. (Meat temperature will rise 5°F during standing.) Remove and discard strings. Slice meat. Makes 6 servings.
PER SERVING *201 cal., 10 g fat (2 g sat. fat), 83 mg chol., 347 mg sodium, 1 g carb., 0 g fiber, 0 g sugars, 27 g pro.*

CHEESY GARLIC POTATO GRATIN

CHEESY GARLIC POTATO GRATIN

PREP 25 minutes
BAKE 1 hour 30 minutes at 350°F
STAND 10 minutes

1½ lb. medium Yukon gold or other yellow-flesh potatoes, thinly sliced
⅓ cup sliced green onions or thinly sliced leek
2 cloves garlic, minced
1 tsp. salt
¼ tsp. black pepper
1½ cups shredded Gruyère, Swiss, provolone, or Jarlsberg cheese (6 oz.)
1 cup heavy cream

1. Preheat oven to 350°F. Grease a 2-quart square baking dish. Layer half the potatoes and half the green onions in prepared dish. Sprinkle with half the garlic, salt, and pepper. Sprinkle with half the cheese. Repeat layers. Pour cream over mixture in dish.
2. Bake, covered, 70 minutes. Bake, uncovered, 20 to 30 minutes or until potatoes are tender and top is golden. Let stand 10 minutes before serving. If desired, sprinkle with additional green onions. Makes 6 servings.
PER SERVING *354 cal., 24 g fat (15 g sat. fat), 85 mg chol., 474 mg sodium, 23 g carb., 3 g fiber, 2 g sugars, 12 g pro.*
Cheesy Garlic Sweet Potato Gratin
Prepare as directed, except substitute sweet potatoes for half the Yukon gold potatoes.

RISOTTO WITH CARAMELIZED ONIONS, BACON, AND MUSHROOMS

PREP 40 minutes
COOK 25 minutes
BAKE 4 minutes at 375°F

2 Tbsp. olive oil
1 cup chopped onion
4 slices bacon, chopped
6 oz. fresh cremini mushrooms or assorted fresh mushrooms, thinly sliced
¼ tsp. salt
⅔ cup dry Marsala
1½ cups Arborio rice
5 cups homemade chicken stock or reduced-sodium chicken broth

RISOTTO WITH CARAMELIZED ONIONS, BACON, AND MUSHROOMS

½ cup freshly grated Parmigiano-Reggiano cheese (2 oz.)
2 Tbsp. unsalted butter
   Black pepper
1 recipe Parmesan Crisps

1. In large deep skillet heat oil over medium-low. Add onion and bacon; cook 6 minutes or until onion is tender and bacon just begins to crisp. Stir in mushrooms and salt; cook 5 minutes or until mushrooms are tender, stirring occasionally. Carefully stir in ⅓ cup Marsala. Cook and stir 3 minutes or until liquid is absorbed. Stir in rice. Cook and stir over medium 2 to 3 minutes or until rice begins to brown. Stir in remaining ⅓ cup Marsala. Cook and stir until liquid is absorbed.

2. Meanwhile, in a large saucepan bring chicken stock to boiling; reduce heat and simmer. Slowly add ½ cup hot stock to rice mixture, stirring constantly. Continue to cook and stir over medium until liquid is absorbed. Add another ½ cup hot stock to rice mixture, stirring constantly. Continue to cook and stir until the liquid is absorbed. Add the remaining hot stock, ½ cup at a time, stirring constantly, until broth has been absorbed. (This step should take 25 to 30 minutes total.)

3. Stir in cheese and butter. Season to taste with pepper. Serve with Parmesan Crisps. Makes 6 servings.

Parmesan Crisps Preheat oven to 375°F. Line large baking sheets with parchment paper. In a small bowl combine 1½ cups coarsely grated Parmigiano-Reggiano cheese, ½ teaspoon snipped fresh thyme, and ¼ teaspoon coarsely ground black pepper. Spoon heaping tablespoonfuls of cheese mixture 4 inches apart onto prepared baking sheets. Pat each cheese portion into a 5- to 6-inch circle. Bake 4 to 6 minutes or until bubbly and light golden brown. Let stand on baking sheets until completely cooled. Carefully remove crisps from parchment paper. Store in an airtight container up to 24 hours or freeze up to 1 month.

PER SERVING 524 cal., 27 g fat (11 g sat. fat), 48 mg chol., 1,311 mg sodium, 43 g carb., 1 g fiber, 2 g sugars, 20 g pro.

CRISPY BRUSSELS
SPROUTS WITH
TOASTED WALNUTS

CRISPY BRUSSELS SPROUTS WITH TOASTED WALNUTS

PREP 15 minutes
ROAST 20 minutes at 425°F

2   lb. Brussels sprouts, trimmed and halved or quartered
¼   cup olive oil
1   tsp. kosher salt
1   cup chopped walnuts, toasted (tip, page 24)
    Shaved Parmesan cheese

1. Preheat oven to 425°F. In a large bowl toss together Brussels sprouts, olive oil, and salt. Spread sprouts on a 15×10-inch baking pan, being careful to not overcrowd.
2. Roast 20 minutes or until browned and crisp-tender, stirring once. Toss with walnuts. Transfer to a serving bowl and top with Parmesan. Makes 12 servings.
PER SERVING *136 cal., 11 g fat (1 g sat. fat), 1 mg chol., 125 mg sodium, 11 g carb., 3 g fiber, 2 g sugars, 4 g pro.*

WINTER PEAR SALAD

Photo, page 128
START TO FINISH 40 minutes

4   cups thinly sliced stemmed kale
2   cups thinly shaved Brussels sprouts
3   pears, halved, cored, and sliced
1   orange, peeled and sliced between membranes into sections
1   cup kumquats, halved
1   cup red seedless grapes, halved
½   cup olive oil
⅓   cup Prosecco or dry white wine
¼   cup white wine vinegar
2   Tbsp. finely chopped shallot
1   Tbsp. chopped fresh chives
2   tsp. Dijon mustard
½   tsp. salt
¼   tsp. black pepper
¼   cup pomegranate seeds (optional)

1. Mix together kale and Brussels sprouts. Arrange pears, orange slices, kumquats, and grapes over greens.
2. For dressing, in a screw-top jar combine oil, Prosecco, vinegar, shallot, chives, mustard, salt, and pepper. Shake well to combine. Drizzle dressing over salad. If desired, sprinkle with pomegranate seeds. Makes 12 servings.

PER SERVING *156 cal., 10 g fat (1 g sat. fat), 0 mg chol., 30 mg sodium, 16 g carb., 4 g fiber, 10 g sugars, 2 g pro.*

BRAISED BELGIAN ENDIVE

START TO FINISH 35 minutes

4   thin slices prosciutto
2   Tbsp. butter
1   Tbsp. olive oil
2   cloves garlic, minced
4   heads Belgian endive, halved
¼   cup apple cider vinegar
¼   tsp. salt
¼   tsp. black pepper
½   cup shredded Gruyère cheese (2 oz.)
½   cup chopped walnuts, toasted (tip, page 24)
1   Tbsp. chopped fresh rosemary

1. Heat a 12-inch skillet over medium. Add prosciutto. Cook 3 to 4 minutes or until crisp, turning once. Remove; crumble when cool. In same skillet melt butter and heat oil over medium-high. Add garlic; cook and stir 1 minute. Add endive; cook 3 to 5 minutes or until browned, turning occasionally. Add vinegar, salt, and pepper. Cover tightly with lid.
2. Reduce heat. Cook 10 to 15 minutes or until the tip of a knife inserts easily into endive. Uncover; sprinkle with cheese. Turn off heat. Let stand, covered, 5 minutes or until cheese is melted. Sprinkle prosciutto, walnuts, and rosemary over endive. Makes 8 servings.
PER SERVING *172 cal., 13 g fat (4 g sat. fat), 19 mg chol., 309 mg sodium, 10 g carb., 9 g fiber, 1 g sugars, 8 g pro.*

BRAISED BELGIAN ENDIVE

GRAPEFRUIT TART WITH CHOCOLATE-ALMOND CRUST

LEMON TIRAMISU

PREP 30 minutes
CHILL 5 hours

- 3 lemons (zest and ¾ cup juice)
- 1 cup sugar
- 2 eggs
- 2 egg yolks
- ½ cup unsalted butter, cut into cubes
  Pinch salt
- ¼ tsp. vanilla
- 2 lemons (zest and ½ cup juice)
- ¼ cup sugar
- ¼ cup water
- ½ cup heavy cream
- 1 8-oz. container mascarpone cheese
- ⅓ cup sugar
- ½ of a lemon, zested
- 12 crisp ladyfingers, halved crosswise
- 8 lemon slices (optional)
  Sweetened whipped cream (recipe, page 91) (optional)

1. For lemon curd, in a medium saucepan combine zest and juice of three lemons, 1 cup sugar, eggs, egg yolks, butter, and pinch of salt. Cook, stirring constantly, over medium until mixture thickens and starts to bubble. Remove from heat. Stir in vanilla. Strain through a fine-mesh sieve. Transfer to a bowl. Cover surface with plastic wrap. Refrigerate 1 to 2 hours or until chilled.
2. For syrup, in a small saucepan combine zest and juice of two lemons, ¼ cup sugar, and ¼ cup water. Heat over medium just until sugar is dissolved. Transfer to a small bowl; let cool.
3. For mascarpone cream, in a small bowl beat cream with a mixer on medium until stiff peaks form (tips stand straight). In a medium bowl beat mascarpone, ⅓ cup sugar, and zest of half lemon with the mixer until smooth. Fold in whipped cream.
4. To assemble, spoon half the mascarpone cream into eight glasses or ramekins (4 to 6 oz.). Dip ladyfinger halves into lemon syrup, coating both sides. Stand 3 ladyfinger halves on the side of each glass. Top with half the lemon curd. Repeat mascarpone and lemon curd layers. Cover servings. Refrigerate at least 4 hours or overnight. If desired, top with sweetened whipped cream and lemon slices. Makes 8 servings.
PER SERVING *533 cal., 34 g fat (19 g sat. fat), 213 mg chol., 85 mg sodium, 54 g carb., 1 g fiber, 46 g sugars, 7 g pro.*

GRAPEFRUIT TART WITH CHOCOLATE-ALMOND CRUST

PREP 45 minutes
BAKE 12 minutes at 375°F
CHILL 3 hours

- 6 oz. whole blanched or slivered almonds
- 3 Tbsp. sugar
- ¼ cup butter, melted
- 3 oz. semisweet chocolate, chopped
- ½ cup butter
- ¾ cup sugar
- 2 Tbsp. cornstarch
- 1 tsp. grapefruit zest
- ½ cup grapefruit juice
- ½ cup orange juice
- ½ cup whipping cream
- 4 egg yolks, lightly beaten
  Whipped cream
  Finely chopped almond slices
  Grapefruit sections

1. Preheat oven to 375°F. Place almonds in a blender or food processor. Cover and blend or process until ground. In a small bowl stir together ground almonds and 3 tablespoons sugar. Drizzle with melted butter; toss gently to coat. Press mixture onto bottom and up the side of a 9- to 9½-inch tart pan with removable bottom. Bake 12 minutes or until golden. Cool on a wire rack.
2. In a small saucepan cook and stir chopped chocolate over low until melted. Spread melted chocolate over bottom of crust.
3. For filling, in a medium saucepan heat the ½ cup butter over medium until melted. In a small bowl combine ¾ cup sugar and the cornstarch; stir into melted butter. Stir in grapefruit zest, grapefruit juice, orange juice, and cream. Cook and stir until thickened and bubbly. Cook and stir 2 minutes more. Remove from heat. Gradually stir about 1 cup hot mixture into egg yolks. Add egg yolk mixture to saucepan. Bring to a gentle boil; reduce heat. Cook and stir 2 minutes.
4. Place saucepan in a large bowl of ice water and stir frequently until filling is cool. Pour filling into baked crust, spreading evenly. Cover surface with plastic wrap and chill 3 to 4 hours or until set.
5. To serve, remove side of pan. Garnish edge with whipped cream and chopped almonds. Arrange grapefruit sections in center. Makes 12 servings.
PER SERVING *380 cal., 29 g fat (14 g sat. fat), 111 mg chol., 103 mg sodium, 29 g carb., 2 g fiber, 24 g sugars, 5 g pro.*

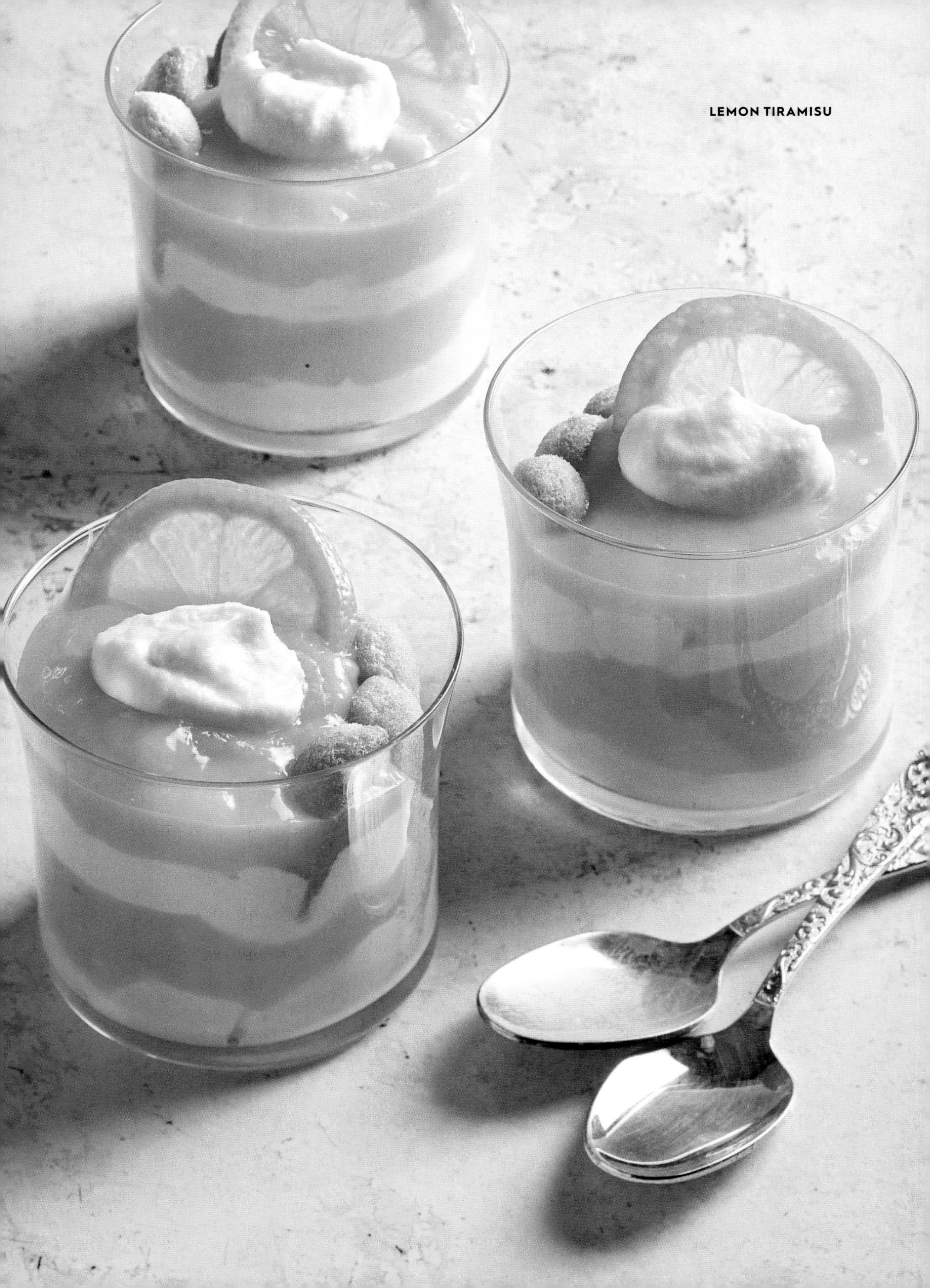

LEMON TIRAMISU

Company's Coming

When you have overnight guests this season, these recipes are perfect relaxed fare. It's fabulous food without the fuss.

ALL-AMERICAN
CHEESEBURGER SOUP,
PAGE 153

APPLE CIDER
ROAST CHICKEN

APPLE CIDER ROAST CHICKEN

PREP 20 minutes
ROAST 1 hour 30 minutes at 425°F
REST 10 minutes

5	lb. whole roasting chicken
1	tsp. kosher salt
½	tsp. black pepper
1	lemon, quartered
10	sprigs fresh thyme
1	lb. sweet potatoes, peeled and quartered
2	apples, cored and quartered
12	prunes
3	shallots, quartered
2	Tbsp. olive oil
2	Tbsp. unsalted butter, broken into pieces
¾	cup apple cider

1. Preheat oven to 425°F. Pat chicken dry with paper towels, then season with ½ tsp. each salt and pepper. Place lemon quarters and half the thyme in chicken cavity.
2. Combine sweet potatoes, apples, prunes, shallots, and remaining thyme sprigs in a 13-×9-inch roasting pan. Drizzle with oil; toss to coat. Sprinkle with remaining ½ teaspoon salt.
3. Place chicken on sweet potato mixture and dot chicken with butter. Pour apple cider in pan and transfer to oven. Bake 1½ hours or until an instant-read thermometer inserted in thigh registers 170°F.
4. Transfer chicken to a cutting board; let rest 10 minutes before carving. Serve with sweet potato mixture; sprinkle with fresh thyme. Pass roasting liquid, if desired. Makes 6 servings.
PER SERVING *507 cal., 23 g fat (6 g sat. fat), 118 mg chol., 330 mg sodium, 36 g carb., 5 g fiber, 18 g sugars, 38 g pro.*

SHORTCUT CASSOULET

SHORTCUT CASSOULET

PREP 20 minutes
COOK 30 minutes
BAKE 20 minutes at 400°F

2	slices bacon, coarsely chopped
1	lb. skinless, boneless chicken thighs, cut into 2-inch pieces
6	oz. smoked pork kielbasa, sliced ¼ inch thick
1	large onion, chopped
2	medium carrots, chopped
3	cloves garlic, smashed
2	Tbsp. tomato paste
⅓	cup dry white wine
1	14.5-oz. can diced tomatoes with basil, garlic, and oregano
½	cup chicken broth
1	Tbsp. herbes de Provence
1	tsp. cracked black pepper
2	15-oz. cans cannellini beans, rinsed and drained
1	cup panko
2	Tbsp. butter, melted

1. Preheat oven to 400°F. In an extra-large, deep oven-going skillet cook and stir bacon over medium-high just until beginning to brown. Add chicken and kielbasa. Cook, stirring occasionally, 6 to 8 minutes or until browned. Using a slotted spoon, transfer meat to a bowl.
2. Add onion, carrots, and garlic to drippings in skillet. Cook and stir until tender, about 10 minutes. Add tomato paste; cook and stir 2 minutes. Add wine; cook and stir 1 minute. Add tomatoes, broth, herbes de Provence, and pepper. Return meats to skillet. Bring to a boil; reduce heat. Carefully stir in beans; bring to a simmer.
3. Meanwhile, in a medium bowl stir together panko and butter. Sprinkle evenly over cassoulet. Bake 20 to 25 minutes or until edges are bubbling and top is browned. Makes 6 servings.
PER SERVING *361 cal., 15 g fat (6 g sat. fat), 62 mg chol., 888 mg sodium, 37 g carb., 9 g fiber, 6 g sugars, 23 g pro.*

TUSCAN LAMB AND WHITE BEAN STEW

PREP 25 minutes
COOK 25 minutes
BAKE 1 hour 40 minutes at 300°F

2	lb. boneless lamb shoulder, cut into 1½-inch cubes
	Kosher salt
	Black pepper
2	Tbsp. canola or corn oil
1	large onion, chopped
2	stalks celery, chopped
5	large cloves garlic, finely chopped
1	Tbsp. finely chopped fresh rosemary
2	Tbsp. all-purpose flour
1	cup dry white wine
1	14.5-oz. can diced tomatoes
1	cup reduced-sodium chicken broth
2	bay leaves
1	15- to 15.5-oz. can cannellini beans, rinsed and drained
½	tsp. honey

1. Preheat oven to 300°F. Pat lamb dry with paper towels and season generously with salt and pepper.
2. In a Dutch oven heat oil over medium-high. Cook lamb in three batches until browned on all sides, 6 to 8 minutes per batch.
3. Pour off and discard all but 2 tablespoons fat from Dutch oven; reduce heat to medium. Add onion, celery, and a pinch of salt. Cook, stirring occasionally, until tender, about 5 minutes. Add garlic and rosemary; cook until fragrant, about 1 minute. Add flour; cook and stir 1 minute. Add wine; cook and stir until thickened and bubbly.
4. Return lamb and juices to Dutch oven. Add undrained tomatoes, broth, and bay leaves. Bring to a boil. Cover and transfer to oven. Cook until lamb is very tender, about 1½ hours. Add beans and honey to stew the last 10 minutes of cooking. Season to taste. Makes 6 servings.

PER SERVING *501 cal., 29 g fat (13 g sat. fat), 93 mg chol., 582 mg sodium, 21 g carb., 5 g fiber, 4 g sugars, 31 g pro.*

TUSCAN LAMB AND
WHITE BEAN STEW

SHEET PAN SAUSAGE
AND FALL VEGETABLES

SHEET PAN SAUSAGE AND FALL VEGETABLES

PREP 20 minutes
ROAST 40 minutes at 425°F

1	small head green cabbage (1½ to 1¾ lb.), cut into 8 wedges through core
¼	cup olive oil
1¼	lb. fingerling potatoes, halved lengthwise
6	unpeeled garlic cloves,lightly crushed
4	fresh sage sprigs
½	tsp. kosher salt
½	tsp. freshly ground black pepper
4	uncooked bratwurst
¼	cup butter
20	small sage leaves

1. Preheat oven to 425°F. Line two baking sheets with foil. In a large bowl toss cabbage in oil, letting excess oil drip back into bowl. Lay wedges on sides on baking sheet. Toss potatoes in remaining oil, letting excess oil drip back into bowl. Place potatoes, cut-sides down, on second prepared baking sheet. Nestle 3 garlic cloves and 2 sage sprigs in each pan, and season with salt and pepper. Cover pans tightly with foil; roast 20 minutes.

2. Remove foil covers from pans. Lightly pierce bratwurst with a fork and toss in remaining oil; add to pan with cabbage. Rotate pans to opposite oven racks. Continue roasting 15 minutes. Turn cabbage, potatoes, and bratwurst; continue roasting until cabbage and potatoes are tender, golden, and cooked through (160°F), about 5 minutes more. Transfer to a large platter.

3. In a small skillet melt butter over medium just until foam subsides. Add sage leaves; cook until butter is browned and nutty and sage is crisp, 30 to 60 seconds. Spoon over vegetables and brats. Makes 4 servings.

PER SERVING *641 cal., 46 g fat (17 g sat. fat), 91 mg chol., 983 mg sodium, 39 g carb., 7 g fiber, 8 g sugars, 19 g pro.*

MUSHROOM AND SPINACH SKILLET PIZZA

PREP 30 minutes
BAKE 18 minutes at 450°F
STAND 5 minutes

2 Tbsp. olive oil
6 cups sliced fresh cremini and/or button mushrooms (16 oz.)
¼ tsp. salt
¾ cup Alfredo pasta sauce
2 Tbsp. grated Parmesan cheese
¼ tsp. dried Italian seasoning, crushed
1 5- to 6-oz. pkg. fresh baby spinach
2 tsp. water
1 recipe Food Processor Pizza Dough or 1 lb. refrigerated pizza dough
1½ cups shredded mozzarella cheese (6 oz.)
Crushed red pepper (optional)

1. Preheat oven to 450°F. In a 12-inch cast-iron skillet heat 1 tablespoon oil over medium-high. Add mushrooms and salt; cook 8 to 10 minutes or until golden and most of the liquid is evaporated, stirring occasionally. Remove mushrooms from skillet. Cool skillet slightly; brush with 1 teaspoon oil.
2. For sauce, in a small bowl combine Alfredo sauce, 1 tablespoon Parmesan cheese, and the Italian seasoning.
3. In a large bowl sprinkle spinach with the 2 teaspoons water. Cover with a plate and microwave 45 seconds; toss. Microwave, covered, 15 seconds more or just until wilted. Let stand, covered, 2 minutes. Chop spinach and place in a sieve; press out excess liquid.
4. On a lightly floured surface, roll Food Processor Pizza Dough into a 14-inch circle. Transfer to prepared skillet and roll down excess dough to form edge of crust. Brush dough with remaining 2 teaspoons oil and spread with sauce. Drain any liquid from mushrooms. Top sauce with mushrooms and spinach. Sprinkle with mozzarella cheese and remaining 1 tablespoon Parmesan cheese.
5. Cook pizza over medium-high 3 minutes. Transfer to oven and bake 18 to 20 minutes or until crust and cheeses are lightly browned. Let stand 5 minutes If desired, sprinkle with crushed red pepper. Makes 6 servings.
Food Processor Pizza Dough In a food processor combine 2 cups all-purpose flour, 1 package active dry yeast, 1 teaspoon sugar, and ½ teaspoon kosher salt. With processor running, add ⅔ cup warm water (120°F to 130°F) and 1 tablespoon olive oil; process until a dough forms. Remove and shape into a smooth ball. Place in a lightly greased bowl, turning once to grease surface of dough. Cover and let rise in a warm place until double in size (45 to 60 minutes). If not using right away, wrap dough in plastic wrap coated with nonstick cooking spray and place in an airtight container. Refrigerate up to 24 hours or freeze up to 3 months. Let chilled dough stand at room temperature 30 minutes or thaw frozen dough in refrigerator before using.
PER SERVING *374 cal., 16 g fat (6 g sat. fat), 40 mg chol., 871 mg sodium, 40 g carb., 2 g fiber, 3 g sugars, 15 g pro.*

MUSHROOM AND
SPINACH SKILLET PIZZA

SQUASH AND SAUSAGE GNOCCHI

PREP 20 minutes
COOK 25 minutes

1   lb. bulk Italian sausage
2   Tbsp. olive oil
1   cup chopped onion
1   2-lb. butternut squash, seeded,
     peeled, and cut into ½-inch cubes
     (4 cups)
1½   Tbsp. chopped fresh sage or
     1½ tsp. dried sage

2½   cups water
½   tsp. salt
1   lb. shelf-stable potato gnocchi
4   cups baby spinach
½   cup freshly grated Parmesan
     cheese

1. In a Dutch oven cook sausage
until browned; remove from pot and
set aside.

2. Add olive oil, onion, squash, and
sage to Dutch oven. Cook over medium
heat 10 minutes or until vegetables are
tender, stirring occasionally.

3. Add the water and salt; bring to
boiling. Stir in gnocchi; reduce heat and
simmer, uncovered, 3 minutes or until
gnocchi float to the top.

4. Stir in sausage and spinach until
spinach is wilted. Serve in bowls topped
with Parmesan. Makes 6 servings.

PER SERVING *521 cal.,
30 g fat (10 g sat. fat), 63 mg chol.,
1,123 mg sodium, 45 g carb., 3 g fiber,
3 g sugars, 18 g pro.*

AVGOLEMONO SOUP

AVGOLEMONO SOUP

PREP 10 minutes
COOK 20 minutes

2 Tbsp. extra-virgin olive oil
¾ cup chopped onion
8 cups chicken broth
1 cup dried orzo
  Salt and black pepper
4 eggs
½ cup fresh lemon juice
2 cups shredded cooked chicken
  Chopped fresh dill

1. In a 4-quart Dutch oven heat olive oil over medium. Add onion and cook until softened, about 5 minutes. Add chicken broth and bring to a boil. Add orzo and cook until tender, 8 to 10 minutes. Season to taste with salt and pepper.
2. Meanwhile, in a medium bowl whisk together eggs and lemon juice. Slowly add 1 cup of the hot broth to the egg mixture while whisking. Then slowly stir the egg mixture into broth in Dutch oven. Add chicken. Cook and stir

until nearly boiling, 1 to 2 minutes. (Do not boil.)
3. Season to taste with salt and pepper, and top with dill. Makes 6 servings.
PER SERVING *316 cal., 12 g fat (3 g sat. fat), 166 mg chol., 947 mg sodium, 27 g carb., 1 g fiber, 4 g sugars, 24 g pro.*

ALL-AMERICAN
CHEESEBURGER SOUP

ALL-AMERICAN
CHEESEBURGER SOUP

PREP 20 minutes
COOK 25 minutes

1   lb. ground beef
½   cup chopped onion
½   cup chopped celery
2   cloves garlic, minced
2   Tbsp. all-purpose flour
2   14.5-oz. cans lower-sodium beef
    broth
2   medium potatoes, coarsely
    chopped
1   14.5-oz. can diced tomatoes,
    drained
8   oz. American cheese slices, torn
1   6-oz. can tomato paste

¼   cup ketchup
2   Tbsp. Dijon mustard
1   cup whole milk
6   cocktail buns, split and toasted*
    Assorted condiments (pickles,
    onions, lettuce, mustard, and/or
    ketchup) (optional)
    Hot french fries (optional)

1. In a large pot cook beef, onion,
celery, and garlic over medium until
meat is browned and vegetables are
tender. Drain off fat. Sprinkle flour over
beef mixture; cook and stir 2 minutes.
Stir in broth and potatoes. Bring to
boiling, stirring occasionally; reduce
heat. Simmer, covered, about 10 minutes
or until potatoes are tender.

2. Stir in tomatoes, cheese, tomato
paste, ketchup, and mustard. Cook and
stir until cheese is melted and soup
comes to a gentle boil. Stir in milk;
heat through. Top toasted buns with
condiments and serve with soup. If
desired, top soup with hot french fries.
Makes 6 servings.

*Tip To toast buns, preheat broiler.
Place split buns, cut sides up, on
a broiler pan. Brush lightly with
1 tablespoon melted butter or olive oil.
Broil 3 to 4 inches from heat 1 minute or
until lightly toasted.

PER SERVING 556 cal.,
30 g fat (14 g sat. fat), 97 mg chol.,
1,682 mg sodium, 43 g carb., 5 g fiber,
14 g sugars, 29 g pro.

CURRIED ROAST AND CARROTS

WILTED RED CABBAGE SALAD WITH PANCETTA AND FETA

START TO FINISH 45 minutes

- 2   medium fennel bulbs with tops
- 3   to 4 oz. very thin pancetta (Italian bacon) slices, or 4 slices lean bacon
- ¼   cup thinly sliced leek or 2 large green onions with tops, thinly sliced
- 1   clove garlic, minced
- ¼   cup dry sherry, red wine vinegar or vinegar
- 2   Tbsp. honey
- ½   tsp. dry mustard
- ¼   tsp. freshly ground black pepper
- 1   lb. red cabbage, cored and shredded (about 4 cups)
- ½   cup crumbled feta or blue cheese (2 oz.)

1. Finely chop fennel fronds to measure 2 tablespoons; set aside. Trim, core, and quarter fennel bulbs. Cut bulbs crosswise into thin slices.
2. In an extra-large skillet cook pancetta over medium 5 to 8 minutes or until browned and crisp, turning once. Using a slotted spoon, remove pancetta, reserving 2 tablespoons drippings in skillet (add salad oil, if necessary). Drain pancetta on paper towels; crumble.
3. Add fennel, leeks, and garlic to reserved drippings in skillet. Cook and stir over medium until fennel is tender. Remove skillet from heat. Slowly stir dry sherry or vinegar, honey, dry mustard, and pepper into drippings. Return skillet to heat. Bring to boiling. Add cabbage; 2 to 3 minutes or until heated through.
4. Top servings with pancetta, feta cheese, and feathery fennel tops. Makes 6 servings.
PER SERVING *126 cal., 5 g fat (3 g sat. fat), 16 mg chol., 252 mg sodium, 13 g carb., 2 g fiber, 9 g sugars, 5 g pro.*

CURRIED ROAST AND CARROTS

PREP 30 minutes
SLOW COOK 8 hours (low) or 4 hours (high)

- 5   medium carrots, cut into 2-inch pieces
- 1   lb. boiling onions, peeled, or 2 cups chopped onion
- 1   1½- to 2-lb. boneless beef chuck pot roast
- ½   cup apple juice or water
- ¼   cup mango chutney
- 2   Tbsp. quick-cooking tapioca
- 1   Tbsp. curry powder
- ½   tsp. ground coriander
- ½   tsp. five-spice powder
- ½   tsp. salt
- 3   cups hot cooked couscous or rice

1. In a 3½- or 4-quart slow cooker combine carrots and onions. If necessary, cut roast to fit into cooker. Place meat on top of vegetables. In a small bowl combine the next seven ingredients (through salt). Pour over meat. Cover and cook on low 8 to 10 hours or on high 4 to 5 hours.
2. Transfer meat and vegetables to a platter. Skim fat from juices. Serve meat, vegetables, and juices with couscous. Makes 6 servings .
PER SERVING *461 cal., 21 g fat (8 g sat. fat), 103 mg chol., 335 mg sodium, 41 g carb., 4 g fiber, 13 g sugars, 26 g pro.*

WILTED RED CABBAGE
SALAD WITH PANCETTA
AND FETA

Index